PELICAN BOOKS
Water in Great Britain

Celia Kirby graduated from Leicester University in 1962, and
then began a government information career with the Ministry of
Technology. From there she moved to the Department of Education and Science, and then to the Agricultural Research Council.
She has published articles in the *New Scientist* and similar journals,
and has written an account of hormone weedkiller development,
published by the British Crop Protection Council. Celia Kirby
now works for the Natural Environment Research Council at the
Institute of Hydrology in Wallingford.

Celia Kirby

Water in Great Britain

Penguin Books

PENGUIN BOOKS

Published by the Penguin Group
27 Wrights Lane, London w8 5tz, England
Viking Penguin Inc., 40 West 23rd Street, New York, New York 10010, USA
Penguin Books Australia Ltd, Ringwood, Victoria, Australia
Penguin Books Canada Ltd, 2801 John Street, Markham, Ontario, Canada l3r 1b4
Penguin Books (NZ) Ltd, 182–190 Wairau Road, Auckland 10, New Zealand

Penguin Books Ltd, Registered Offices: Harmondsworth, Middlesex, England

First published 1979
Revised edition 1984
10 9 8 7 6 5 4 3

Made and printed in Great Britain by
Richard Clay Ltd, Bungay, Suffolk
Filmset in 10/12 pt Monophoto Bembo

Contents

Preface

I wrote most of this book during the very wet and miserable year that followed the hot, dry and uncomfortable summer of 1976. Memories are amazingly fickle: watching the rain slashing down it was hard to recapture the feeling of helplessness with which only a few months previously colleagues and I had discussed the 'whats' and 'ifs' of one of the most severe droughts that this country has ever experienced. It is capricious behaviour of this kind which makes water such a fascinating subject. This book is about how we come to terms with it to provide water for the nation.

Considering that we only use about a tenth of all the water that falls as rain, it seems ludicrous that on occasions we can actually run out. Conversely, flood insurance claims account for millions of pounds each year.

Along with air and food, water is a resource we cannot do without. But not only for fundamental biological reasons is water vital to mankind since we use it in so many different ways, from drinking and washing to cooling and transport. The surprise is that we have managed so well for so long given that growing demands have never yet been matched by adequate financial support. At least, that is what the industry itself says about its problems.

Water authorities have to borrow very heavily indeed to meet their commitments. These include not just water conservation and supply, but also sewerage and sewage disposal, the control of water pollution, land drainage and flood prevention, recreation, fisheries and some inland navigation. Much of the cash flow is devoted to replacement of existing antiquated networks especially in the older urban areas. And whereas it was water supply that preoccupied the industry in the late seventies, it is now the dirty end of the business that figures most prominently in costing exercises. The biggest problem is ageing sewers – difficult to locate, sometimes impossible to inspect, and highly disruptive when they fail – all are agreed that this is where most effort will be concentrated in the next decade.

There seems to be little public sympathy for the water industry. This, I suspect, is mainly because of the low rates for water paid by consumers in the past without any real conception of what they are buying, since the raw material is not only free but also indestructible.

So what exactly does the public get for its money? Let us take a close look at what is involved in supplying clean water to and taking water away from where people live or work. We must also look at the options available and note prevailing official attitudes, which sometimes see water supply and disposal solely in terms of a public service. But water is a national resource and as such, and in our use of it, it has environmental as well as industrial constraints which we ignore at our peril.

October 1983   Celia Kirby

List of Text Figures and Maps

List of Tables

I *The Basic Problems of Water Management*

Everyone knows that water from a tap is the stuff that falls as rain or snow, flows down rivers and comes up from wells. The difference is that we expect to be able to drink tap water neat. Making sure that it is safe to do so is one of the main things we pay water rates for. They cover two interrelated services: a supply of good clean water to drink, wash in, water the garden with, and then its disposal when we have finished with it. Both these services rely on underground pipe networks which make it easy to forget where water comes from or where it goes.

Mains water supply is based on three types of source. Depending on the nature of the terrain and the level of demand, water from your tap may have come from just one or a combination of two or even three of these. Simplest of all, many water boards take their supply from the local river. Other regions rely on catching rain in reservoirs, of a size depending on the area they serve and how often it rains. Finally some lucky areas extract water from underground reserves, part of the deep-lying natural water table. The water industry is skilled at balancing between the three sources, switching from one to another when possible, so that water is always available.

But shifting water about costs money. To move water means using energy-intensive pumps and accounts for much of the current price of water. Even so, it is still the cheapest commodity there is. Nor are we going to use it up in the way fossil fuels are being irreplaceably consumed. It comes and goes and comes again without any help or hindrance. We can use it and abuse it but never destroy it. Regrettably, there are times when there is not enough to go round. This is when the non-essential uses must be curtailed and we get hosepipe bans. Is this through sheer bad management or niggardly capital expenditure? The water authorities say they have to walk the tightrope between spending too much on expensive extra storage facilities not used in 'normal' years, which make water costly, and not spending enough so that restrictions become too frequent to be acceptable.

More than any other public utility water has suffered from an extraordinarily complicated bureaucracy. Since water is a very common and important substance, many different parties, local authorities, water supply boards, sewage boards , river authorities and three government ministries have had responsibility for different parts of the water cycle. Some of the undoubted overlaps have been re-moved in recent reorganization of the industry, but it is too soon to say whether pointless duplication of effort has been eradicated en-tirely, since modification to the overall plan continues to be made, albeit often with political overtones.

At least we have moved away from local administration and now plan strategy on a regional basis. This at last makes it possible to consider the interactions of water with our existing social and environ-mental framework, and to take positive steps to avoid damaging our surroundings by being careless about where we put our waste. For the tantalizing feature of the water industry is that most of the prob-lems relate to the dirty end of the business. So much of the disposal network, particularly the sewers under towns, was built with no design consideration at all, both in relation to capacity and to the places where they were to discharge their contents. Many were formed simply by enclosing existing streams and letting them carry their noisome contents into the main river channels. It is easy to understand the reasons behind this neglect of sewer development. When so much of the water cycle was part of the local government machinery it suffered from the democratic system; there are no votes in sewerage.

High standards of reclamation matter not just because of improve-ments in the amenity value of the environment but also because the reuse of water is so important on grounds of efficiency. As soon as water planners became regionalized, it made sense to use the natural waterways as the basis for distribution. There is no point in pumping water from distant reservoirs through pipelines when it will flow unaided down a river through gravity. But although logistically a better solution, such newer management techniques put a strain on the operators. They must guard more rigorously against pollution and must judge releases from upstream reservoirs according to likely weather patterns.

The basis of all water planning is the extrapolation from past events coupled with projections in demand. Weather forecasting is still in its infancy, however, and despite more sophisticated computer modelling of global air circulation, it is not likely ever to be sufficiently specific for small areas or over sufficient timespans to help the water planner. Even now cynics argue that current weather forecasts are the best we are ever likely to get, simply because the climate is in a state of flux and has been ever since the earth had an atmosphere.

Given the added complication that accurate demands for expansion in water services are not likely to be predictable far enough ahead (it takes ten to twenty-five years to implement new supplies) local water shortages are inevitable from time to time when freak weather patterns work against us. How often, how severe and how prolonged these droughts are will depend on what happens from now on. A good downpour soon relieves the worst effects of a drought but unfortunately it also washes away much of the interest in providing against the next dry spell, and makes it hard to drum up support for contingency plans.

No one yet knows the full sociological or economic implications of droughts. How much effort is applied to water resource planning and management now will affect the patterns of society in the future. One thing is sure: the control, supply and disposal of water will continue to play their part in changing the face of these islands.

2 *Water, Water Everywhere*

Talk to any visitor to Britain and you find he expects to see the entire population wearing plastic macs or carrying rolled umbrellas. Indeed, all school fête organizers know to their cost that this pessimistic attitude towards our weather is often justified. On a world scale the British Isles get only a middling amount of rain annually, but our geographical location is such that what we do get is spread very evenly throughout the year. What the meteorologists call an equitable climate, the general public calls unpredictable; very few realize that in fact there is a severe drought in the UK at least once every five years.

The mechanism of rainfall is just one part of the dynamic water cycle operating throughout the earth. The forces which keep the cycle turning ignore political boundaries and obey no international rules. Water is truly a global resource. The amount of water in the earth's crust and in the atmosphere is three times the quantity of all other materials combined. Oceans, ice caps, glaciers, lakes, rivers, soils and the atmosphere contain some 1,500 million cubic kilometres of water in one form or another. Nearly all of this volume, some 97 per cent, is the saltwater of the oceans, which cover three-quarters of the earth's surface. Three-quarters of the remaining 3 per cent is locked up in the polar ice caps and in glaciers. The rest is mostly deep-lying groundwater. The tiny fraction left over is continually recycling: precipitation equals evaporation, at an overall world rate of 1,000 millimetres a year as measured in our rain-gauges.

Fortunately for us land dwellers there is an imbalance, with the oceans losing more water by evaporation than they gain from rainfall. This small portion of freshwater is sufficient to support terrestrial life, although sometimes only with a struggle; water, like many other vital natural resources, has a very uneven global or regional distribution. The volume flowing in rivers is minute as a percentage of total water at any given time, but it is the fount which keeps us all alive for the bulk of the world's liquid freshwater supply is impounded in lakes.

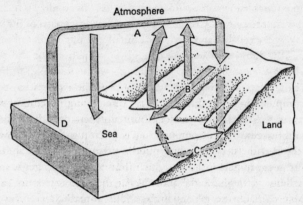

Figure 1 Water Cycles. Water is continually moving – under the force of gravity as rainfall, runoff and percolation and in rising and horizontal air currents as vapour. Storage occurs as a dynamic equilibrium between gain and loss at four main points: (A) in the atmosphere, (B) on the surface in rivers, lakes and as ice and snow, (C) underground in aquifers and (D) in the sea.

Accurate estimates of available freshwater reserves are hard to come by. The difficulty is the constant increase and depletion through precipitation and evaporation, much of which occurs over the oceans where there is as yet virtually no way of obtaining actual measurements. This situation may change when the esoteric indirect information we now get via satellites becomes quantifiable and available on a small enough scale.

At the same time, how far any theoretical global water balance, put together from mathematical principles, actually relates to existing or future needs is not known either. This is because we just do not know how to calculate the effects of social factors influencing growth in demand for water supplies or the regional boundaries; conventional resource planning for currently available supplies to meet future requirements cannot anticipate future economic or technological changes. But water will never be exhausted, as other resources may be in time. Planners take comfort from the premise that as the demand for water grows so it will be satisfied by recycling. Just as the extrapolation of demand can be projected to infinity, so can the number of recycling processes be assumed to be infinite.

Our equitable maritime climate means that this country is relatively rich in water resources. Compared with many other parts of the world we have very reliable and frequent rainfall – about 1,000 millimetres a year (the long-term annual average precipitation for the period 1941–70 is 1,090 millimetres*). Although we may lose up to half of this rainfall input almost straight away through evaporation during the summer months, this still leaves an annual average of 780 millimetres, equivalent to 515 million cubic metres a day. Current demand figures for water supplied by the water authorities are some 16 million cubic metres (16,250 cubic metres a day in 1982). Translated to a more personal scale, this means that if we caught all the rain falling we should have about 800 gallons of water for each of us every day. On average, we use about 26 gallons (120 litres) in our homes, although total consumption per head of population is 64–6 gallons (290–300 litres) per day because of water used in factories, for fire-fighting, leakages, etc.

With all this surplus rainfall, why then do we have water shortages? Out of this apparently vast supply we have to allow for several important and severe losses. First, there is the need to keep rivers at prescribed levels so that they function as navigation channels and can support the indigenous fish and plant life. This is done by adjusting the depth with weirs in dry weather or letting as much water as possible run out to sea when the rivers are running at full spate in the winter. In both instances a great deal of water flowing away downstream cannot be abstracted for use. Even when there is spare water available, a certain amount is lost through inefficient pumping or leaking pipes.

Much more serious is the wide regional and seasonal variation

*Precipitation is defined as any aqueous deposit, in liquid or solid form, derived from the atmosphere. For records, frozen precipitation is melted before measurement. The rain-gauge measure of liquid or melted precipitation is the depth to which the ground would have been covered had no run-off, percolation or evaporation occurred.

both in demand and supply. South-east Essex, for example, with an average rainfall of 250 millimetres can lose nearly twice this amount through evaporation in a dry summer, which makes very heavy demands on abstraction from underground sources or reservoir storage. Further, we are stuck with the geographical feature of rather short rivers, so the water falling as rain over the source areas will therefore go out to sea only a few days later.

Atmospheric water vapour, from which the rain comes, never reaches more than 40 per cent by volume of the air above, the total being less than one two-hundredth of all global freshwater. However, as our islands are surrounded by sea there is always a fair amount of water vapour up in our sky. Turning that vapour into rainfall depends less on the precise amount of moisture in the air than on favourable rainmaking conditions. Unlike liquid water, water vapour is considerably lighter than dry air. Therefore water evaporated from the earth's surface rises and is cooled by its ascent into colder air to form clouds made up of minute droplets of liquid water which grow in size by turbulence and by condensing on solid particles – specks of dust, etc.

What actually triggers the rainmaking process depends on the vertical movements of air masses. A parcel of air can hold a certain amount of water, depending on its temperature: the higher the temperature, the more it can hold. Cool the parcel of air and it will eventually become saturated and hold no more. Cool it a little more and rain must fall. Air parcels are cooled because, and only because, they are made to rise. Their pressure drops, they expand, and so they cool.

There are three mechanisms which make them rise. First there is the land configuration. Westerly winds carry warm wet air from the Atlantic to hit the mountains of Scotland and Wales. It is forced up into cooler air and the water condenses and falls. This is called 'orographic' rainfall and is the major influence on our rainfall pattern. This is also why a map of annual rainfall of Great Britain looks very much like a relief map. Second comes the structure of our familiar 'depressions'. In these, warm air from the west is again forced to climb, but this time over colder air forcing itself underneath from the north. This is a dynamic travelling system. As the whole travels across the country, the rain belt, called the warm front, travels with

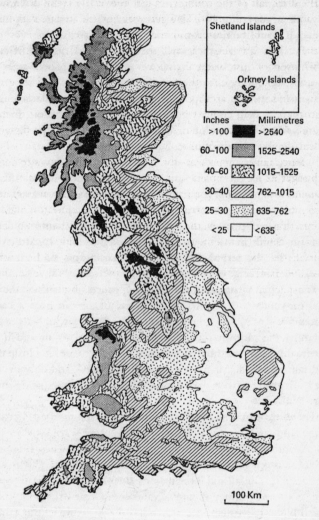

Figure 2 Mean annual precipitation over Britain between 1916 and 1950.

it. The third mechanism is what causes most of the rain falling over the drier east of the country, called 'convective' rainfall. If, on a hot summer's day, an area of land gets very hot, the air parcel immediately above it will be heated and rise, like a hot-air balloon. As it meets the cooler air above it will rise faster and faster, building up atmospheric instability, often over a large area. The weather forecasters then announce the familiar 'widespread thunderstorms over such and such an area'. Convective rainfall is particularly important in the planning context because, out of all proportion to the total amount of this type of rainfall, it is often both unpredictable and 'extreme' over a short time.

Since rainfall represents the gross income in the water engineer's budget its measurement is of crucial importance. Rainfall measurements are made using a gauge whose dimensions were standardized in 1866. Rain-gauges are basically a simple funnel to collect water into a receiving vessel, the amount of water collected being expressed as the depth (in millimetres) to which the ground would be covered if all the rain stayed where it fell. Rain-gauges do no more than sample rainfall at a point and although there are some seven thousand rain-gauges throughout the UK, of which about six hundred are

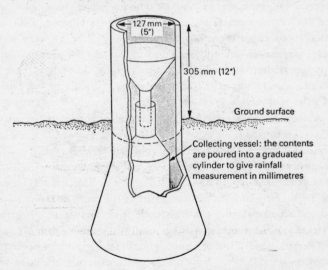

Figure 3 Rain-gauge – standard Meteorological Office pattern.

at official meteorological stations, this averages out at one in every 40 square kilometres. Also, most of the gauges are in lowland sites rather than on high ground where more of the rain falls, for high ones are much more difficult to service. Despite their dubious accuracy, however, many of the records go back to the last century and so provide invaluable information about seasonal trends.

Altitude is the main factor deciding amounts of rainfall over the land surface. Roughly speaking, there is an 8 per cent increase over sea-level totals for each hundred-foot increase in elevation. Of course this is an over-simplification: there are local variations where prevailing winds or exposed slopes get more – south-west slopes can experience up to four times more rain than equivalent north-east facing slopes, for example. And again, unexpected gains come from purely convectional storms formed by local heating.

When talking about rainfall incidence, meteorologists usually compare the current situation with 'average' annual rainfall. This is complicated, however, for statistically the climate changes over a period of time. For example, the thirty-five-year period 1916–50 was some 4 per cent wetter over the country as a whole than the previous thirty-five-year period 1881–1915. For parts of Scotland, the difference was as much as 14 per cent. These relatively long-term trends are not very noticeable on a year-to-year basis because of the wide fluctuations about the mean rainfall. As we all know, very wet or very dry seasons are followed sooner or later by excesses of the opposite extreme. Looking at the records, it appears that the occasional very wet years are balanced by a slightly higher number of years with below average rainfall.

Average annual rainfall figures for a country with such varied topography as ours, sitting as we do right in the path of major global circulation currents, cannot reflect regional differences. Years which produce up to 5,000 millimetres of rain over the high ground in the Lake District, Snowdonia and the west of Scotland yield a mere 500 millimetres or so in the driest part of the south-east. Yet records from the home counties (for example from Harpenden, Hertfordshire) show that over a ten-year period 45 per cent of days are 'wet', that is, had at least 2 millimetres of rain. Indeed, most of the country's meteorological stations show little obvious pattern in the fluctuation of either seasonal or monthly rainfall, to the extent that if records

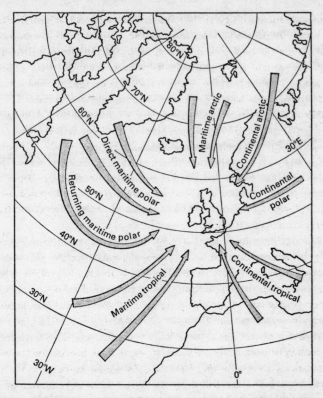

Figure 4 Trajectories of principal air masses affecting the British Isles. 'The weather of the British archipelago depends heavily upon imported air though its outstanding characteristics, moisture and moderation, may be regarded as at least partially home-brewed since they arise from the nature of the surrounding seas.' Crowe P. R. (*Concepts in Climatology*, Longman, 1971.)

are examined over a long enough period, it is possible to find that every single month of the year at some time has been the wettest and at another the driest month of any individual year. It turns out that there are very few places which have not recorded a 100 milli-metre daily rainfall (which is a fifth of the annual total for Cam-bridgeshire) at least once in the last hundred years. Nevertheless, in the north and west the highest monthly totals of heavy rain occur in the winter, while in the south-east the highest monthly totals of heavy rain are for July and August because of convectional storms.

The most important fact to emerge from all this statistical information is that, luckily for us, it rains very often. It is this factor that colours our management attitudes to water and the design of our supply systems. The frequency of rainfall, in particular, is all-important, as the following recent instance shows. In 1973 there was a very dry winter followed by a relatively wet summer. This caused problems for the farmers but the weather certainly did not hit the headlines. In 1975, although January, March, April and September had above average rainfall, the rest of the year saw us facing severe water shortage problems. But the surprising thing is that the *annual* rainfall figures indicate that 1973 and 1975 were extremely similar, in that 738 millimetres of rain fell in 1973 and slightly more, some 752 millimetres, in 1975.

The dry winters of the early part of the 1970s, coupled with indifferent summers, gave rise to much speculation about accelerating climatic change. The decline in the frequency of westerly winds blowing across the country undoubtedly influenced the type of weather we experienced. In terms of impact on water management or planning, however, this phenomenon has had little effect so far, since there has been no discernible decrease in the annual rainfall totals that the planners work with. The current spirited debate among climatologists about the existence of fluctuations of the order of mere decades is at least stimulating research programmes to assess the effects of such changes and their implications for future water storage schemes.

The next important consideration is the fate of rainfall. There is a convention that a period of fifteen days or more without rain is an officially recognized drought. But fifteen days without rain in the summer has vastly different consequences from fifteen dry days in winter. To assess whether a dry period should truly be classed as a drought demands some investigation of the condition of the soil. Soil consists of an organic component, humus, together with mineral particles derived from the weathering of rocks. There will be different kinds of particles present, according to the various parent rock origins, and of differing sizes and shapes, which give rise to a variety of soil types. The irregular shapes and sizes mean that spaces are left between the soil particles, allowing the earth to act like a huge sponge, absorbing large amounts of water. How much, and how quickly, depends on the physical make-up of the soil. In general, soils with a uniform consistency conduct water much more rapidly than those where there are layers of different aggregate forms or degrees of compaction.

Particularly important is the physical condition of the soil surface. If the surface becomes compacted it can act as a barrier to slow down the rate at which the water soaks in. During very heavy rainstorms, the water hitting such a surface may flow over the top of the soil instead of soaking in, especially on slopes. This causes severe erosion problems in many parts of the world where rainstorms are more intense than here. Such a crust forms not only under the beating action of raindrops but also through repeated traffic by animals or machinery – hence the ruts filled with water often seen at the entrance of fields in winter. The problems of compaction, resulting in water-logged fields, are worrying many farmers. The last thirty years have seen much farm labour superseded by bigger and heavier machinery, making compaction yet more noticeable, and as the large farm-combines spend lavishly on equipment in their search for higher productivity, so more and more money is spent on extensive land drainage.

Soil devoid of vegetation is not something found very often in a truly natural situation in temperate regions of the world. But bare soils are an indispensable feature of the arable landscape during at least some parts of the year, as when crops are cleared or the soil is prepared for sowing. Such unnatural phenomena change the rate of infiltration of rainwater. Not only do the various cultivation techniques which remove vegetation alter the relative proportions between the total volume of solid particles and pore spaces but they also compact or loosen the whole soil system. Opening up the soil and leaving it in furrows for the winter frost to break up the heavy clods is a well-known technique and has been part of farming practice since ploughs were first used. This helps to produce the fine tilth the farmer wants for his seedbed and permits a freer interchange of water in the topmost layers of soil.

The amount of water in the soil varies most in the first metre or so below the surface. From the driest condition, known as the wilting point, to the wettest drained state – field capacity – may

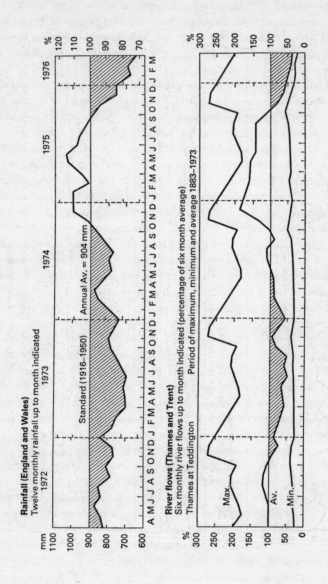

Rainfall (England and Wales)

Twelve monthly rainfall up to month indicated

Standard (1916-1950)

Annual Av. = 904 mm

River flows (Thames and Trent)

Six monthly river flows up to month indicated (percentage of six month average)

Period of maximum, minimum and average 1883-1973

Thames at Teddington

Max.

Av.

Min.

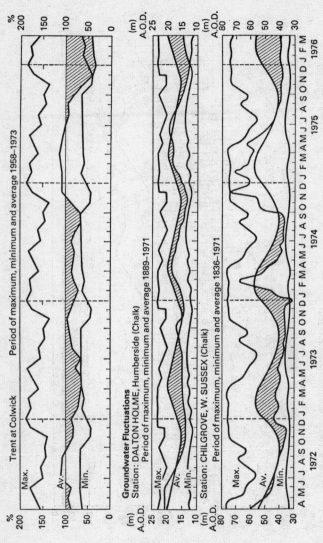

Figure 5 Rainfall (England and Wales), riverflows (Thames and Trent) and groundwater levels April 1972–March 1976, showing the wide fluctuations in yearly water measurements.

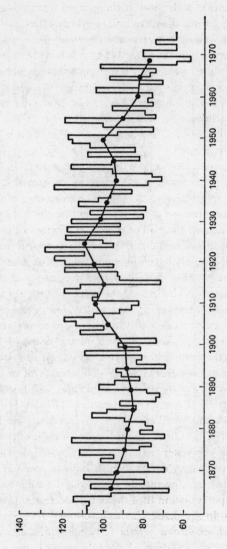

Figure 6 Number of days each year with general westerly winds blowing over the British Isles from 1861 to 1973.

be a rise from 3 to 10 per cent content in a sandy soil or from 20 to 40 per cent in a clay soil. If the ground is waterlogged, as when it is raining harder than the rate at which water is draining away below, then even more water can be present.

Soil generally absorbs water as fast as it rains but under any given set of conditions there is a maximum rate at which it can do so. This depends both on the basic soil properties and on how much water was present initially. These infiltration rates and the extent of the redistribution of water in the soil in turn affect the rate of water and nutrient loss and ultimately the efficiency of the soil to support plant growth.

Two processes determine why water stays in the soil. First, there are adhesive forces between water and the soil granules, second, capillary forces operate, as a result of the narrowness of the soil pores and the surface tension of the water, so that the soil sucks up water like a wick against the pull of gravity. Sometimes these forces bind the water so firmly in the soil that a large part of it becomes almost immovable, certainly beyond the powers of plant roots to abstract.

The soil reservoir is thus a dynamic system. The amount of water present constantly changes as the structure attempts to maintain equilibrium between the upward movement of water through the influence of evaporation and the downward forces of gravity. The amount of water present in the soil usually decreases fairly steadily throughout the summer months as evaporation and uptake by plants exceeds the income from rainfall. This builds up a 'soil moisture deficit' which in south-east England, at least, usually goes on increasing until the end of August or September. This deficit depends firstly on the prevailing weather, which governs both the rainfall 'gain' and the evaporation 'loss', and secondly on the ability of plant roots to forage for the water they need. Deep-rooted trees, for example, can build up a bigger deficit than shallower-rooted grass. However big the deficit gets, eventually there comes a month when rainfall exceeds evaporation and then the deficit decreases, from the surface downwards. In shrinkable clay soils summer drying often produces cracks which go down several feet and which allow the rain to penetrate quickly and deeply before the upper layers are completely rewetted. In general, though, it is not until the deficit has been made good throughout the soil profile that there is any percolation beyond the soil layers to the deep-lying rocks beneath.

The potential water yields from catchment areas are usually assessed on an annual basis and ignore the soil storage component. A water balance is drawn up of the gains and losses, using measurements of rainfall input on the one hand and river-flow records and evaporation losses on the other. If the equation does not balance – and it rarely does – the missing value is assigned to the water that has gone into storage. Such crude calculations have been sufficient for most of the water resources planning of the past. There are now occasions when we need to do better. The wide variation in topography, ground cover, the increasing interference with natural drainage mechanisms, are factors that require actual measurements of the soil moisture present. Considerable research into the mechanisms of soil moisture movement and the uptake of water by plants now figure prominently in hydrological research programmes. The ultimate aim is to refine the predictive equations and so improve the allocation of scarce resources.

The forces of molecular attraction and capillary action holding water in the soil are both strong enough to resist the force of gravity trying to pull the water downwards. A film of water clings to in- dividual soil particles and only the surplus above and beyond that necessary to coat each particle evenly eventually drains down to the regions below. There is nevertheless an awful lot of water beneath the ground – an estimated 8,350,000 cubic kilometres – but this vast quantity has accumulated over the centuries and rainfall infiltration probably contributes very little net gain each year, a point to bear in mind when extensive groundwater abstraction is being advocated for the arid parts of the world.

The level within the subsurface strata below which all the voids between particles are filled with water is called the 'water table'. Above and below this level, subsurface waters are referred to respectively as 'soilwater' and 'groundwater', the latter being the storage component of the water cycle. Soilwater either moves up- wards through the influence of evaporation and abstraction by plant roots, or downwards under gravity. Groundwater, on the other hand, can move in all directions, depending on hydrostatic pressures within the pore spaces. In fact, groundwater is constantly moving, often

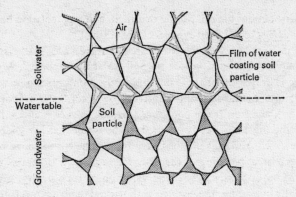

Figure 7 Schematic diagram of soilwater/groundwater interface.

over extensive distances, from areas of recharge to points of discharge. The velocities at which it moves are of course sometimes very slow, maybe only a metre or so per hour or even per year.

Different types of rock have various sizes of space between the particles, and the cracks or fissures that have formed over the ages produce a varying extent of interconnecting passages, all of which can hold water. The ratio of void space to total volume of rock is known as the 'porosity'. But it is not the porosity of a particular rock formation which is most important so far as the water engineer is concerned, because if these void spaces are very narrow the capillary forces will be too strong for the water to be extracted upwards. The permeability (the term which is given to the capacity of rocks to yield water) is therefore a function of the size of the individual rock particles, their shape and packing characteristics, and also the degree of fissuring that has taken place. For example, clay, gravel and chalk each have a porosity of over 30 per cent but the small size of the particles makes clay useless as a water-bearing stratum for resource purposes. Chalk too can be extremely dense but by contrast the high degree of fissuring usually present means that it is a very productive water source.

Any natural stratum that yields water sufficiently easily for it to be exploited for public water supply is called an 'aquifer'. Where aquifers have permeable material above them, the upper saturated

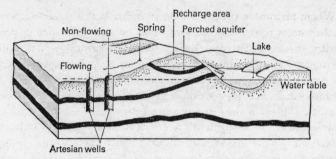

Figure 8 Cross-section of schematic terrain to show how artesian wells function. Impermeable rock strata in black, permeable material in grey.

limit (the water table) is free to follow the topographic contour of the ground surface, rising beneath hills and falling in the valleys. Stream levels will similarly be approximately the same as the ground-water level. When, however, the rock layers above them are impermeable, aquifers are said to be 'confined' or 'artesian'. Wells and boreholes sunk through the impermeable layers into the fully saturated level, at points below the level of other parts of the water table, will flow without pumping because the water is under pressure.

In resource terms, there will be a decrease in yield (that is, the amount of water that can be extracted) with increasing thickness of overlying material. This is largely due to the weight of the rock which compacts the particles in the aquifer material and reduces its inherent porosity. Another serious limitation to yield is an overlying soil that is not very permeable, so that recharge is reduced. Even if good yields were originally possible from such aquifers, the delay in recharge makes them virtually useless as a permanent resource.

When aquifers are 'full', with the rock voids saturated, the excess water flows out through cracks or fissures at the surface, which we call springs. Springs are the natural overflow mechanisms of ground-water stores. Depending where they are in relation to the full height of the aquifer, they will either flow all the year round or only after heavy rain has overtopped the storage potential. During periods of high water levels, springs and streams appear in valleys normally dry at other times. The type of spring-fed stream common in chalk and limestone country is known as a 'bourn', a term often reflected in local places names.

Where permeable rocks occur in river basins this same overflow mechanism is responsible for significant volumes of water in permanent streams and rivers. Because the water has followed a more devious route since falling as rain than has the water draining off the surface, there is a greater time-lag before it forms part of the streamflow. In very dry weather the only water actually flowing in many streams is this groundwater component. Conversely, the replenishment rate of groundwater reservoirs depends not only on rainfall but also on the state of the soil; if it is dry then the falling rain must saturate the soil layers before topping up the aquifer levels. The slope of the land becomes important: the steeper the slope the more efficient the runoff, and the less water there is to infiltrate the soil. Rainfall intensity also plays an important part in determining recharge rates, moderate to gentle rainfall being better than heavy thunderstorm downpours. The latter tend to saturate the top layers of the soil very quickly and form a crust on the surface.

The most important type of aquifer in this country is that formed by the large deposits of chalk roughly stretching south of a line between Weymouth and the Wash, plus parts of east Yorkshire and Lincolnshire. The chalk supplies about 40 per cent of the groundwater abstracted for the public supplies. Chalk near the surface or outcrop area amounts to some 12,950 square kilometres and geologists estimate at least a further 18,000 kilometres at varying depths below the soil. Its thickness ranges from 90 metres to 500 metres and although very fine-grained it is extremely porous, largely due to countless fissures. These will transmit water to wells in considerable quantity; wells sunk in fissured zones have been known to yield up to ten times more water than from nearby non-fissured areas.

The other major groundwater exploitation zones are the regions of the Bunter and Keuper sandstones. These geological deposits outcrop over some 4,532 square kilometres with probably another 3,237 square kilometres underground. These aquifers have been most developed in the Midlands and because they have a high permeability, there are only small seasonal fluctuations in the water level. Furthermore, the effective thickness of the sandstones is greater than the chalk and there is no doubt that they have great potential for future water supplies. For example, the upper 50 metres of the saturated Bunter sandstone which outcrops in Nottinghamshire

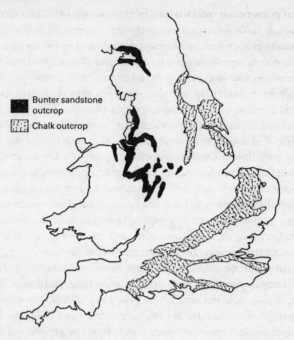

Figure 9 The two main waterbearing strata in the UK – the Chalk and Bunter sandstone.

contains over nine million million litres of available water, about five times the total amount of water stored in surface reservoirs throughout the country.

The potential yield of an aquifer depends on two factors. The first is the amount replenished annually through rainfall infiltration. The second is the storage component, the water lying below all natural outlets and therefore not depleted by droughts. Estimates of the extent of the water available are calculated from the thickness of the aquifer and its permeability. Unless the aquifer is to be 'mined', which is damaging in the long term since it is using up non-renewable resources, it is the replenishment volume that is important to the water engineer. In gross terms, the amount likely to be available each year is reckoned to be the difference between mean annual rainfall and actual evaporation over the area of the outcrop of wherever recharge is taking place. With such a simplistic approach, errors can arise, especially in the south where the two values are very similar in some years. A constant check has to be kept on well water levels to monitor the seasonal fluctuations.

None of the statistics related to water resources have any real meaning when they are expressed as averages for the country as a whole because of the range of climatic and topographic features within these islands. This is particularly true when talking about evaporation losses. The return of water to the atmosphere is controlled by solar radiation, temperature, humidity, wind speed, soil texture and type, and density of plant cover. Evaporation rates also vary with the depth to which the ground is saturated and above all depend on whether or not there is any water there to evaporate: evaporation figures for sunny periods during the 1976 drought were exceptionally low, because the water had all gone from the top layers of the soil.

Apart from the movement of the water molecules away from the liquid surfaces of rivers, reservoirs or even from puddles in the road, there is also evaporation loss via plants through the process known as 'transpiration'. Under optimum growing conditions, the pores of the leaf surfaces are fully open so that carbon dioxide can diffuse into the cell tissues for the metabolic process of photosynthesis. In these circumstances water vapour wafts out, at a rate governed solely by the physical controls of sunshine, temperature, humidity and ventilation. As a leaf loses its water (transpires), it develops a suction which has the effect of drawing water through the plant, a movement which begins with absorption of water from the soil through the roots. The transpiration process can use up water in the soil down to the lower limit of root penetration.

The riddle is to know how plants maintain the balance between keeping the leaf pores open enough for maximum carbon dioxide uptake, necessary for growth, and closing them sufficiently to prevent excessive water loss and wilting. The warm atmospheric conditions favouring the latter are also those most conducive to peak growth rates. When the supply of water gets low, the amount of water transpired by a plant varies from species to species because of different internal cell structures and it is possible to detect changes in the daily cycle of leaf-pore closure. Normally, though, a state of equilibrium exists within the plant between absorption from the soil, of water within the plant, and transpiration to the atmosphere. A plant may transpire several times its own weight of water on a hot summer's day. Thus what the water engineer tends to call 'loss' is the working capital of agriculture.

The other form of evaporation loss which must be taken into account is what is known as 'interception'. When it begins to rain the falling droplets mostly land on the surface of vegetation before sliding off to reach the ground. As all who have sheltered under a tree know, depending on the intensity and duration of the passing storm, a proportion of the water landing on the leaves stays there, to be evaporated back into the atmosphere in due course. This inter- cepted rainfall, which never reaches the ground at all and thus short- circuits the usual water cycle, is now known to be a significant component of the water budget. It is thought to be sufficiently sig- nificant to warrant research into quantifying the different amount of interception loss associated with different types of vegetation. For instance, water caught by a forest canopy with its large surface area of branches, twigs and needles or leaves can total as much as 40 per cent of the incoming rainfall, compared with perhaps only 10 per cent held by grass or short crops in open fields.

Evaporation is virtually impossible to measure directly. As it is the point in the water cycle where liquid water changes into vapour, it demands an energy supply – the sun's radiation – for the necessary heat of vaporization. But secondly, the process also depends on the rate at which molecules of water vapour are moved away from the surface of the water, and so aerodynamic factors such as wind speed, atmospheric turbulence and humidity come into play. Evaporation figures are got either from direct measurement with evaporation pans (simply containers of water which are topped up each day, the amount of water needed to bring the level back to the norm assumed to be equivalent to the water evaporated during the previous twenty- four hours) or from formulae incorporating measurements of climatic variables.

Evaporation estimates are important for water engineers when cal- culating the water available from their catchment areas. High rates of evaporation during the summer mean that most rainfall input only satisfies the soil moisture store and average flows in the rivers; very little surplus will drain down to recharge aquifers or find its way to man-made storage reservoirs. At times of severe drought an under-standing of the evaporation component becomes crucial to avoid damaging over-exploitation of sources. The generalization values which assume that evaporation loss is consistent seasonally and over all types of vegetation and which suffice for annual estimations just will not do in these circumstances. The detailed assessments of evaporation which are possible in a research context show that evaporation loss is underestimated, particularly during the winter months, and that the existing equations in use should be weighted for areas with extensive tree cover to take proper account of inter-ception.

Farmers too become very concerned about evaporation losses in the form of transpiration rates. They do not have to do the cal-culations themselves but are guided by the MORECS service operated by the Meteorological Office. MORECS stands for Meteorological Office Rainfall and Evaporation Calculation Scheme, and takes the form of a weekly bulletin giving estimates of actual evaporation, what is termed 'hydrologically effective' rainfall, and soil moisture deficit. It is a computer-operated system which uses data on the meteorological variables extracted daily from the Synop-tic Data Bank at the Meteorological Office's Headquarters at Brack-nell (input originally from the 125 synoptic weather stations all round the country) and from which weekly values are derived on the day of issue of the MORECS bulletin. The values are given for each of a 40 × 40 km square grid over the whole country; see Figure 10.

The conventional techniques for assessing evaporation loss assume that the only control is the atmosphere's evaporative demand. But this will not always be the case because, unless rainfall is abundant, the soil is not always wet enough for water to be readily available to plants. Opinions vary on whether potential and actual transpiration are the same (i.e. whether the figures for evaporation loss computed from formulae agree with what is actually lost in real situations) or whether the plants themselves are able to control water loss. There is certainly a growing volume of evidence that during dry periods the actual losses are less than the values expected from

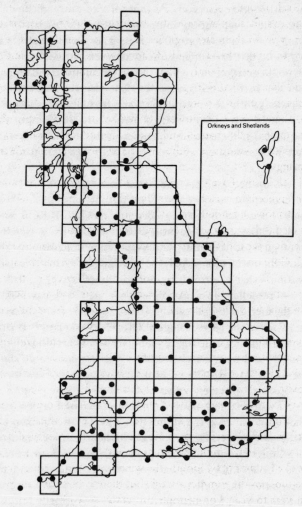

Orkneys and Shetlands

Figure 10 The MORECS grid and locations of synoptic stations.

calculations. More research is needed here because of the great practical benefits to projected irrigation needs that could arise from refinements in the calculations.

The output side of the water balance is the crucial part of the water cycle for the water engineer. It is his net cash flow, from which he has to budget his demands. Water flowing in streams and rivers has several origins. Firstly, there is surface runoff – the proportion of rain that flows directly over the surface of the ground and into the channel, plus the water that actually falls into the channel itself. Then there is what is known as interflow, the moisture in the soil which drains to the channel, and finally, in some geologically favoured locations, a groundwater component from the underlying water table or springs.

The volume of water in rivers at any one time depends entirely on the preceding weather conditions. Climatic factors, such as the combination of amount and duration of rainfall, tend to have the greatest influence on the broad monthly regime, making winter levels higher than those of the summer months. Shorter fluctuations depend much more on the physical characteristics of the particular catchment areas.

Runoff ratios, which give streamflow expressed as a percentage of rainfall, vary considerably over the country. Most of Scotland and mid-Wales are able to boast values of over 80 per cent while south-east England can do little better than 30 per cent. This regional difference is why it is hard to say precisely which is the largest river in the UK. On a catchment area basis the Thames comes out on top with an area of 9,868 square kilometres, but the River Tay has over twice the discharge of the Thames, produced from a catchment area of only 4,584 square kilometres. The Tay is thus an example of a river draining an area with high rainfall and low average evaporation rates, reflected in the high runoff ratio.

Looked at month by month, the winter maximum values are about twice those of the summer runoff, but these values vary enormously from year to year. For example, in wet years with say 125 per cent of average rainfall they may be as much as 95 per cent of average annual discharge, but dry years with only 80 per cent rainfall may yield a mere 54 per cent runoff. This is why years only a little drier than normal can easily lead to drought conditions because the lower runoff ratios aggravate the situation. Also, any groundwater input can do funny things: thus, for example, in the dry summer of 1975 despite the fact that the rainfall was way below average, figures for streamflow in rivers with a substantial groundwater contribution were much higher than average, entirely due to the storage built up during the previous wet winter.

Gauging stations on rivers became mandatory under the 1948 River Boards Act but there are some records which go back many decades – the Thames has been gauged at Teddington since 1883 and the Lea spasmodically at Fieldes Weir since 1851 – but there is no historical archive of streamflow records comparable to the records given in the annual publication *British Rainfall*, which dates from 1861. *Surface Water – U.K.* is the newest equivalent reference book, first published in 1938 and covering the period 1935–6. The latest edition, the twentieth, covers the period 1977–80.

How much water there is in a river depends on how deep the river channel is and how fast the water is flowing. The first measurement is usually easy: a permanent staff-gauge with depth markings is a common sight near locks and weirs. Velocity measurements with a current meter are not so simple because the velocity of the water is not the same at all points in the river. Several readings have to be taken to find an average value. Likewise, cross-sectional area depends on soundings taken right across the bed to find the depth and distances from a fixed reference point on the bank. Depth soundings are particularly difficult in silt-laden or weedy rivers where it is hard to decide exactly where the boundary is between the firm bed and the semi-fluid layers immediately above.

Unfortunately, current meters do not work at velocities of less than 150 millimetres per second and many British rivers, including the Thames and the Great Ouse, for example, normally flow much more slowly than this. Other limitations are the tediousness of the large number of readings needed on wide rivers and the uncertainty of any measurements in unsteady flow conditions especially during flooding or where releases are being made from locks. This is why wherever possible special structures are built where the water is funnelled through a narrow uniform cross-section trough or over sharp-crested weirs.

The more sophisticated gauging installations with permanent level recorders can send telemetered information back to control points so that sluices can be operated by remote control for general river management. However, sometimes it is impossible to build a gauging structure, either because the river is too wide, or because of problems with navigation, or simply for aesthetic reasons, so that *ad hoc* readings with a current meter have to suffice.

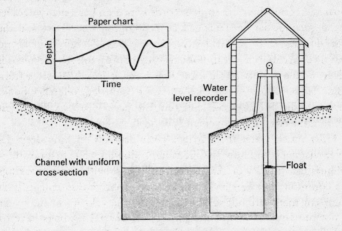

Figure 11 Principle of river level measurement in permanent gauging structures.

Like other hydrological measurements then, riverflow figures have a wide margin of error. Consequently using records taken over only short periods to assess potential yield is extremely dubious, but since extensive river gauging in many instances only goes back to the early sixties, that is all we have to go on.

We must now see how these sources of supply are exploited by water engineers to provide the public with adequate amounts of safe water at all times.

3 From Source to Supply

The possibility of a three-day week for industry at the height of the 1976 drought in those regions where water was in short supply really brought home the message that water is a basic need of society. For many people this came as a nasty shock, judging by the way the news media responded. The idea that a commodity should cease to be available simply at the whim of a fickle climate was hard to accept. No labour relations to blame, no over-optimistic forecasting to pinpoint. Nothing, except the cold reality that delays in implementing sufficient storage capacity, through financial constraints or environmental controversy, had caught us napping in a 1000-to-1-against freak weather pattern.

Many senior water management executives admitted that they were dismayed by the indignity of resorting to standpipes. They regarded the original 1847 Act relating to piped water supply as a kind of gospel decreeing that priority should be given to clean water supply for the people at all times. This was primarily on health grounds. Early legislation made no provision for industry to take piped water except in special circumstances. That top priority should now be given to industry – that they should get the piped water – and domestic consumers asked to go without, was seen as a violation of the water engineer's prime duty. Communal standpipes in the streets had overnight put the clock back a hundred years.

The rapid expansion of towns in the industrial revolution put great strains on the supply of unpolluted water which mostly came from local streams. Even before this, many towns had had to use the services of water carriers to take water supplies round on hand carts in those districts without wells or pumps. The extreme overcrowding in city tenements provoked the most virulent outbreaks of disease, the causes and intensity of which had for centuries been known to have a connection with water: as far back as Tudor times, Thomas Cromwell had set up authorities to do something about the quality of London's water.

An example of a scheme well in advance of its time was that launched in 1622 by one Hugh Myddelton, who constructed the 'New River', an artificial channel bringing water from the springs in Ware, Hertfordshire, to a reservoir at New River Head (now the site of the Thames Water Authority's headquarters in Clerkenwell). From there the water was taken in lead pipes to the City of London. On a wide scale not much happened until the nineteenth century, because there were only spasmodic outbreaks of really serious diseases such as cholera related to water. This was not brought from the areas where it was endemic, simply because the journey took so long that boat crews infected with it died *en route*. Matters got worse as communications improved, but once water was identified as the culprit measures were swiftly taken, such as the separation of sewerage from drinking water supplies, provision of sewage farms and closure of polluted wells.

Incidentally, the spread of the 'black death', bubonic plague, the most dreaded disease of medieval times, was indirectly connected with water. It was spread by rats; bad weather caused flooding and drove the infected rats into town centres away from their usual haunts in the dockland areas; the weather kept people tied to their rat-infested homes, increasing the chances of infection.

Victorian engineering prowess soon made it possible for water to be piped to individual households on a national scale. A mixture of private enterprise and public benefaction implemented water supply schemes all over the country, the bulk of which are still operating today. In essence, clean water was allowed to collect in natural or artificial basins well away from possible contamination and then fed through pipes to consumers. Naturally the extent of the network varied with the terrain of the area and the ambition of the operators.

The large cities of the Midlands and the north-west, expanding rapidly in the last century, were at first able to rely on fairly local sites for their storage reservoirs. Gradually, as demand grew, they were forced to look further afield. Cities like Birmingham, Liverpool and Manchester now enjoy the legacy of the foresight of early city fathers who invested wisely in the reservoir schemes in the mountain areas of the Pennines, Wales and the Lake District. Who can fail to be impressed by the splendour of the dams and pumping houses on Lake Vyrnwy and the Elan Valley reservoirs, for example, which hold water for cities some fifty miles away. But as well as being proud of their engineering achievements, we should bless these early engineers for their contribution to the nation's welfare. It is said that there has been more benefit to health from a wholesome public water supply than from the whole of medical science.

All water supply schemes based on storage work in the same simple way. Suitable valleys are turned into reservoirs by damming the main streams and allowing the basin to flood up to a safe level. Their large volume means that some reservoirs take several years to fill, but once full the water draining into the valley through natural processes replaces the water taken out for use.

There are violent and conflicting views about the aesthetic appeal of artificial bodies of water. But quite apart from such considerations, it is the dam structure on any reservoir which commands the most immediate attention, whether it be the Wagnerian style of those built in the last century or the most self-effacing attempts to merge with the landscape that characterize modern structures. This is especially so when one knows that dams, like icebergs, only expose a part of their total bulk to view. The vast stresses imposed by the ponding up of millions of gallons of water demand some of the most exacting engineering design calculations of our time. This, coupled with the cost of such an undertaking, makes a new reservoir proposal no mean task, apart from the time and expense involved in meeting all the demands of the environment lobby and the inevitable public inquiry.

Dams can be built of earth, rock, concrete or masonry, the choice of material dictated by the geology of the site and by their different costs. Concrete or masonry dams need firm rock foundations but earth dams can sit on clay or other strata that are sound. The key factor in all dam construction is to make the foundations watertight. As the reason for building a dam is to hold back water in the valley behind it, the site chosen must be one with stable geology so that the valley itself is watertight, at least up to the highest intended water level. Comprehensive geological surveys are needed to check for faults or permeable strata; ignorance of the geology of the valley sides has regrettably led to some terrible dam disasters because excess water in the reservoir has put an intolerable strain on the hillside.

The water taken out of reservoir storage for supply to a town is drawn off some way back from the dam and flows by gravity through pipes to treatment works on the outskirts of the town. There are usually several points at different levels from which it can be taken, since the surface level changes, and the best point is about halfway down. This is because the water tends to remain stratified in layers, with the water which arrived most recently on top. This layer is therefore likely to contain a fair amount of sediment or organic matter, precise quantities of which will change with time – most sediment eventually falls to the bottom and organic particles are consumed by bacterial action. The bottom-most layer, on the other hand, will probably consist of water that has been in the reservoir for a long time and may be rather foul and stale. This natural, self-purifying process undergone by water stored in bulk means that in many cases reservoir water is fit to drink after only minimal filtration and the addition of a little chlorine.

Most water authorities own the land surrounding the reservoir, the 'gathering grounds' or catchment areas, and to safeguard the purity of their water, they used to impose strict limitations on the kind of farming allowed and also prevented public access at all times. Recent concern about leisure pursuits and a better appreciation of the countryside has led to a certain amount of relaxation but even now no swimming or water sports of any kind are allowed on some reservoirs. This kind of restriction, coupled with the fact that probably as much as three-quarters of all the water in upland reservoirs is stored for use many miles away from the source area, has caused some political problems in Wales, whose population see the export of Welsh water to England as the exploitation of a resource over which they have no control and from which they get no financial gain. It is a bitter pill to swallow when south Wales suffers from water rationing during dry summers because of minimal capital investment in storage schemes during past boom industrial growth periods. Restricted access is also regarded as a severe national amenity loss in many National Parks where, as in the Peak District, for example, a third of the area is occupied by reservoired catchments.

At one time there was a swing away from building reservoirs, mainly on cost grounds, towards abstraction from rivers, though money then had to be spent on treatment plants. Water for the public mains is taken out of rivers at specially constructed intakes, either by ponding up the river with weirs or by taking it in through a floating pontoon. Abstraction must be possible at all times yet not interfere with river users. The amount of water that can be taken out of a river to meet the consumer demand depends on how much needs to be left behind so as not to upset the biological regime of the river, to leave a sufficient depth for navigation and for the adequate dilution of the effluent from sewage works – it is often forgotten that we rely on our rivers to take away the 'used' or dirty water when we have finished with it.

The minimal freshwater flow needed at the tidal estuary must also be considered, otherwise the tides will in time increase the saline content of the riverwater further back upstream and so interfere with the quality at the established abstraction points. A certain level of freshwater is moreover counted on to dilute the effluents from industries which have been specially sited for this very purpose downstream.

A cardinal rule in modern water resource management is to make rivers stay as rivers, to keep sufficient water flowing for all the river's normal functions. Always maintaining the flow above a set minimum level means that upstream users benefit from the extra water present in dry seasons. The other side of the coin is the need to keep levels down during wet periods so that soil drainage mechanisms operate normally, otherwise waterlogged fields would become a nuisance.

Extensive use of riverwater for drinking is only possible if the quality remains high. For this reason there are plans to ensure that in future all river abstraction points will be able to cope with seven days' storage. This will allow abstraction to be stopped immediately should there be any unforeseen pollution, such as an accidental spillage of toxic wastes from a local factory. It will also allow proper monitoring of the quality of the water on a continuous basis before it gets into the distribution mains (not yet universal practice) and will probably bring about a limited quality improvement through settling and self-cleansing.

The deteriorating quality of riverwater plus the problem of inadequate natural flow to meet peak seasonal demands have more recently brought reservoirs back into favour. Reservoirs are now being designed to be part of a whole river system, with the function of storing water for regulating the flow in the river. This allows the natural river channel to be used as the chief distribution artery and saves on costly pipe installations. It also makes it easier to take the water out close to the individual points of demand. The newer philosophy of water resource management is thus to make the natural water pathways work for us, by delaying and storing water on its otherwise headlong rush from the hillsides to the sea.

Storing water ready to top up inconveniently low rivers during dry spells is not a new idea. Header ponds, as they were called, were formerly a common feature of water mills, and reservoirs were also built adjacent to rivers or canals that had important navigational functions to be protected. Without such man-made storage there are times, especially in the summer, when the only flow in a river after a long dry spell is the natural water seeping out from under-lying aquifers. In the vast majority of rivers this natural minimum flow amounts to a mere 10 per cent of the average streamflow and is often a lot less. On its own without some kind of regulation this would be quite inadequate for navigation, let alone for water abstraction. The dry weather flows of our rivers today are effectively double the natural minimum levels because of the storage/regulation systems already in operation, even though the quantity of water held in store to make this possible is only equivalent to about 20 per cent of an average year's runoff.

Dry weather flows could be increased even further. They cannot, however, increase indefinitely, for although rivers are dangerously low for only relatively short periods, and flows can be greatly improved by releasing quite a small volume of water, there is a limit to the number of times in a season that valuable stored water can be used in this way. Reservoirs would have to be enormous if they were expected to release unlimited amounts of such compensation water. There comes a point when it is more economic to improve the quality of effluents, or to change their point of discharge to one further downstream, making a lower freshwater flow acceptable, than to keep on adding extra storage to keep the flow large enough. Water engineers think it unlikely that regulation schemes will go beyond the point at which dry weather flow is pushed up to more than 40 per cent of average flow. The Thames, however, may have to be an exception to this rule because of the extensive demands made on it all along its length.

Given the enormous expense involved in construction costs, there are very clear advantages in building reservoirs to regulate rivers rather than to supply direct by aqueduct, always provided the quality standards can be successfully upheld. In the river regulating reservoir there is much more water available to meet the different abstraction demands than from the same volume of storage held for direct supply. This is because the whole of the basin draining down to the river along its entire course contributes to the flow, whereas a reservoir behind a dam is fed only by the upland areas above it. Furthermore, successive abstractors can reuse the same water as it passes downstream, and there is greater flexibility in allocating sources to demands. It takes some getting used to, but it is a fact that Thames water, for instance, is used about six times between Oxford and Teddington.

The correct size for individual reservoirs, whatever the ultimate fate or function of the water, depends not only on the storage capacity but also on the way the water cycle operates in each particular location. This affects the initial filling of the reservoir and its recovery rates if large quantities of water are abstracted over a short period. The calculations necessary incorporate past rainfall records for the catchment area, the performance of the streams which will feed the reservoir, and water levels in aquifers which might influence the water yield of the catchment.

The storage so designed can never guarantee unlimited stocks. That is impossible. What the design engineer tries to achieve is sufficient storage to yield a certain predetermined or prescribed flow plus enough spare capacity to meet a level of demand likely to occur, on average, not more than once or twice in a hundred years. There is no reason why extra storage capacity should not be provided but since this would be needed on even rarer occasions, the cost/benefit sums are so horrific that all such proposals get vetoed at an early stage.

Water is released from regulating reservoirs when the level at the abstraction point furthest downstream is the lowest that will maintain 'minimum acceptable flow', a predetermined fixed amount. Examples of rivers which are now operated in this way are the Dee, the Severn and the Tees. A choice of storage facilities within a river system allows flexibility in the management options available during times of stress. It might happen, for example, that one reservoir is kept in reserve and all releases made from the other(s), or a little let out from each, depending on the time of year and state of the storage levels within the whole river catchment area.

Allowing for flood alleviation is often a vital constraint on the operation procedure of river systems. Normally it means making sure that the autumn levels are low enough to leave room for the winter floodwater. The Clywedog reservoir on the upper Severn has its level drawn down deliberately by 1 November each year to give a flood retention capacity of 1,850 million gallons (about $8\frac{1}{2}$ million cubic metres). Then, over the winter, the level is allowed to rise until it reaches the optimum for the summer by 1 May. A delicate balance is required in some years to get the level right, for if the winter is dry, reservoirs are likely to be called on to augment low flows early in the summer season, and could then be dangerously low for their longstop functions during the rest of the summer.

Some reservoirs refill rapidly with runoff from the catchment, and can change from being half empty to bankful in a matter of weeks; others respond more slowly and many need the help of pumps to divert water from the rivers in the area. The complications of flood control, water quality, recreation and general appearance (who wants to walk the dog along mudflats on a summer afternoon?) preclude the chance of operating some systems in either the cheapest or the simplest way.

This greater flexibility in the way we exploit our rivers and marshal our water reserves produces clearcut benefits over the earlier type of direct supply system, but there is no denying that such schemes are costly. All types incur operational losses, which means providing more storage than the volume actually needed. Pumping from a river into a reservoir for later use is, for example, expensive in power demand and involves loss of water. If this water, moved with difficulty and expense, is then not needed because sufficient rain falls soon after, it must be written off as a total loss. But deciding not to husband any surplus when it is there, on the offchance that the weather will come to his aid at the right moment, is a gamble that the river engineer dare not take. It is fair to say that as yet we have little real experience of the extent of operating losses in these river regulation schemes, in terms of what they add to the annual water bill. When calculating expected yields, arbitrary allowances are made to account for what is held in the channel itself, for seepage into and through the banks and riverbed, and for the inadequate coordination of releases both in quality and time, which is bound to happen even without interference from the weather.

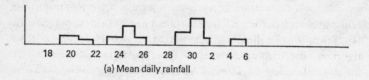

(a) Mean daily rainfall

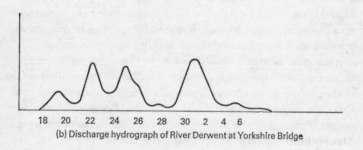

(b) Discharge hydrograph of River Derwent at Yorkshire Bridge

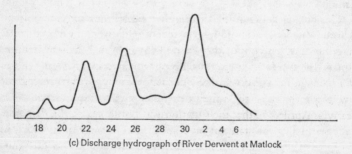

(c) Discharge hydrograph of River Derwent at Matlock

Figure 12 Reservoir storage used for flood protection. Floodwater resulting from three heavy rainstorms in January 1960 (a) was largely absorbed by reservoirs at Yorkshire Bridge (b) but once these were full (on 29 January) the level of the Derwent rose rapidly further downstream at Matlock (c).

In some cases the opportunity for river regulation using reservoirs sited upstream may not be feasible and what are known as pumped storage reservoirs are built. These are favoured for lowland sites near to abstraction points on the lower reaches of a river. As the name implies, they are filled by pumping water out of the river during the winter high flows or after storms. Like the upland storage reservoirs they have an inherent advantage in that the water is likely to be of a reasonable quality, since impurities tend to fall out of suspension when water stands for a while. This puts a lighter load on the purification plants than on those which have to deal with water directly from the river. The lovely clear water from Llyn Celyn in north Wales, for example, loses a good deal of its pristine quality in its two to three days' journey down the River Dee to the abstraction point near Chester, placing a great strain on the waterworks for Liverpool and Birkenhead. By contrast London's supply network includes thirteen bankside storage reservoirs. These keep the water much purer in the course of its journey.

After periods of dry weather, when water is getting scarce, contingency plans come into operation, to ensure that the flow at the intake point is regulated relative to the amount of water left in the reservoir or in the river. At least in theory, then, the reservoir can never run dry or the rivers get so low as to become stinking sewers. This problem of meeting minimum acceptable flow levels presented extreme difficulties in the dry summers of 1975 and 1976 and legal action had to be taken to cope with the emergency. The Drought Orders which were rushed through Parliament were not only to allow water authorities to impose severe restrictions on non-essential use, but also for them to be allowed to cut back on the minimum levels they are required to maintain in rivers. That it requires Parliamentary intervention to alter river levels and to restrict their use is a measure of the sanctity of water supplies. It was known as early as April 1976 that the situation was bordering on the desperate but because of the statutory operating rules in force many millions of litres were irretrievably lost before the emergency powers to husband the dwindling stocks remaining could be implemented.

The lessons learnt from this episode were obvious in 1983, when a few hot summery weeks in July saw stringent water restrictions being imposed despite the fact that the early part of the year had been extremely wet and water resources were plentiful, a reaction interpreted by many as unduly hasty.

For some time it has been argued that as it is the residual flow after abstraction which is the important criterion, it ought to be possible to allow a little leeway in the regulations to operate the system on a two- or three-day running average, so that any deficiency one day could be made up the next and vice versa. It seems most unlikely that anyone would detect the difference in the river itself, especially since the majority of flow measurements are only accurate to within 15 per cent, even in ideal conditions.

Many areas get their water directly out of the ground from wells and boreholes, tapping sources first exploited during the early stages of industrialization. This is particularly true in the south and east where the Chalk aquifers provide a constant and plentiful supply.

Like many natural surfacewater sources, most groundwater supplies were developed originally to serve purely local needs, to give continuous direct supply. Many of them are now being used more effectively for intermittent river regulation, or in combination with a surface source. This reflects the newer philosophy of integrating resources for complete geographical areas. Certainly some existing groundwater sources could be better used in this way and no doubt will be altered along these lines in future.

Up to 35 per cent of the water used for public supply in England and Wales (only 5 per cent in Scotland and Northern Ireland) comes from groundwater sources. For all that, it is probably the least appreciated of our national water resource heritage. There is some water under the ground nearly everywhere, and providing it is not too deep, it can be extracted fairly easily. The oldest and cheapest method is of course the simple dug well which goes back to biblical times and beyond. Traditional wells range from ten to forty feet deep. For safety, they need some kind of lining of wood, brick, rock, concrete or metal, always with openings to allow water to seep into the well. The well shaft usually goes down a few feet beyond the normal water table to allow for seasonal fluctuations in level.

Water at a greater depth is extracted from boreholes. These are drilled in a variety of ways, depending on the depth and size of shaft, those used for commercial extraction being obviously more complex than say, single boreholes for farm use. Seldom more than six to

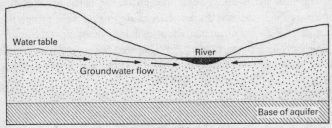

Natural conditions

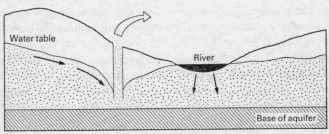

Borehole near stream

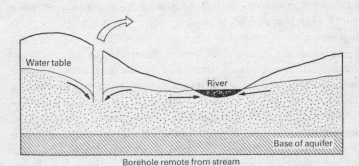

Borehole remote from stream

Figure 13 Methods of groundwater extraction.

eight inches in diameter and up to fifty feet deep, boreholes work best in soil or rock formations that are firm enough not to cave in.

Large-scale groundwater exploitation demands the installation of large, deep, high-capacity wells which need the services of a specialized drilling crew to form large diameter shafts, often up to four feet in diameter. The performance of a new well is checked and double-checked through lengthy pumping tests. The prime purpose of such tests is to find the potential yield, the efficiency with which water collects in the well. Also important is the need to note changes in the quality of the water and any regional upsets such as the lowering of levels in nearby wells. Most tests are done in the autumn when the levels are at their lowest. Wells are tested by first measuring the static water level and then pumping at the maximum rate possible until a new stable level is achieved. The difference in depth is called 'drawdown' and the discharge/drawdown ratio is an estimate of the specific capacity of a well.

Once the shaft has been sunk, the well has to be developed so that it will perform at maximum efficiency whatever the nature of the rock strata. Sands and gravels tend to be open and loose, and while usually stable in their natural state, are easily compacted when disturbed by drilling. The permeability and porosity in the vicinity of the well may, however, be restored if the fine grained material produced by drilling is removed from the walls of the shaft. The pumps for extracting the water are slung in position at a level at which they will still be submerged when the water table is at its lowest during the year.

Although the location and overall dimensions of major aquifers are known fairly precisely, there is still room for a certain amount of exploration and survey work, especially where new sources are required or existing well fields are to be modified. Modern geological survey uses the sophisticated techniques of electrical resistivity or seismic methods for estimating the thickness and extent of water-bearing gravels and to locate buried channels in bedrock.

Only rough estimates, based on experience, of the potential yield of new sites are initially available. In fissured aquifers especially it is a chancy business whether large amounts of water are struck or not. Even in the usually reliable sand aquifers a change in the pattern of the clay deposits above can drastically reduce the effectiveness of

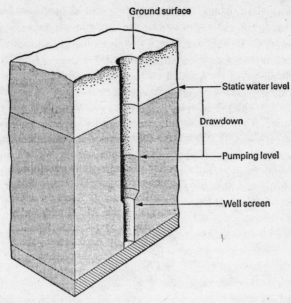

Figure 14 Measuring well performance.

a well. It is this chance element that makes the drilling of a small observation borehole at a major site so crucial. Even so, a good yield from this will not guarantee good yields from the main well, and if it failed it might put off the development of what could in fact be a very good site.

Complete information on well levels is very important in building up a picture of what lies beneath the ground surface. For this reason records of any borings which go down below 30 metres must be reported by law. A national record of well levels is kept by both the British Geological Survey and the Institute of Hydrology at Wallingford. These records give information not only on levels but also on where salt contamination has been found in wells near the coast. This type of information helps in understanding the distribution and movement of the vast stores of underground water against the time when they might be needed.

So how much water can be got out of a commercially productive well? In the Chalk, wells can be over a metre in diameter and as much as 100–140 metres deep. Such wells can yield in excess of three million gallons a day. Wells in the Triassic sandstones are smaller and are often developed as a group of wells connected to one pumping station, collectively producing up to five million gallons daily. The Lower Greensand which outcrops around the margin of the Weald and the north-east of the London basin in Bedfordshire and Cambridge-shire are important groundwater sources, as is the limestone of the Cotswolds with prolific yields if there is extensive fissuring in the rock formation. Finally, there are the carboniferous limestone outcrops in the Mendips, the Peak District and north-east Yorkshire, which are rarely developed for water supplies on their own although they sometimes form part of combined schemes in which the water comes from both storage reservoirs and from wells.

Not nearly enough is yet known about the physics of water move-ment in the ground. What is certain is that water deep down behaves in a strange fashion. Hydrogeologists know that beyond some depths water movement ceases completely and for this reason it is not worth drilling below 150 metres, and better to attempt increased yields by enlarging the diameter of the shaft. Why this is so, research work has not yet answered.

Water in the environment is normally in a state of dynamic equilibrium. The abstraction of groundwater, however small, upsets the balance, and changes in storage and runoff take place as the system returns to equilibrium. The consequences of limited abstraction are not usually noticeable because the volume of water held as ground-water is vast compared to the amount being taken out. There have been instances where the accumulated effects of extensive abstraction from several wells does become apparent, with possibly a fall in well levels and a reduction in riverflows. In severe cases, the ground can subside and near the coast there can be the problem of well water becoming too salty to drink. In these coastal aquifers there is a natural gradient with the freshwater running out to sea. Freshwater and salt-water have different densities, seawater being heavier than fresh. Because of this, freshwater stays above the saltwater and the boundary between the two layers advances and recedes according to changes in seasonal runoff, tidal variations or with excessive pumping.

As there is such a large volume of water stored in the soil and as it takes a long time to flow through the subsurface strata, it is some time before really damaging effects become apparent; it is the job of the water resources engineer to make sure the over-exploitation stops before such drastic effects occur.

Early groundwater developments primarily took advantage of the permeability of aquifers, which allowed water to flow to the well or wells at the desired rates; in other words the aquifer itself was used as a giant pipe. With continued development the actual volume of water stored in the rocks has nevertheless begun to decline to a significant extent in many areas. This has made it necessary to think hard about the long-term usefulness of groundwater supplies and has increased the emphasis on integrated schemes using both surface and groundwater.

The Stocks reservoir in the north-west of the Yorkshire border which drains the Bowland area of the Pennines was originally built as a direct supply source which, together with water pumped from the Bunter sandstone, supplied Blackpool and the Fylde region. Each source produced about 55 million litres a day, i.e. some 110 million litres in total. Managing the two sources as a single supply, however, means that it is often possible to meet 75–80 per cent of the demand from the reservoir alone instead of on a 50–50 basis, a much better operational technique in this instance because water from this source happens to be cheaper to treat and transmit. The next stage in water resource development for this area is to step up abstraction from the Rivers Lune and Wyre, knowing that there is backup storage in both the reservoir and the aquifer to meet demand even under 1-in-a-100-year drought conditions.

Other examples of new integrated developments are the exploitation of groundwater from the Lincolnshire limestone in combination with extraction from the Rivers Welland and Nene, the Shropshire sandstones with the River Severn, the Triassic sandstone of Nottinghamshire with the Rivers Dove and Derwent, the Vale of York sandstones with the River Ouse and the East Yorkshire Chalk with the River Hull. Just how far such conjunctive use schemes will go is an open question. A conservative estimate puts the contribution of groundwater sources as 30–40 per cent of total water supplied by the end of the century, roughly the same proportion as at present. One point to bear in mind is that it may be mistaken policy to put good quality groundwater into rivers where it first has to dilute sewage effluent.

Water from wells usually needs less treatment than river or reservoir water. This is because it comes already filtered, having passed through subsurface gravels during its transition from rainfall to groundwater. In effect, we take it out partway through a conventional treatment cycle, when it has been filtered to an extent not ordinarily possible in man-made plant. Surface waters are much dirtier, being vulnerable to gross contamination. They are likely to require some or all of the following treatments – coagulation, sedimentation, filtration, softening, disinfecting, correction of corrosiveness – before they are fit to drink. Some lake or reservoir water, particularly from upland sites, may only need disinfection, but as a safety precaution all waters are filtered. Groundwaters are often clear and although they may need some softening or iron removal, usually have little need for the taste or odour improvement which may be necessary with surface-waters.

Flowing water usually has fine particles of silt or clay held in suspension. If such riverwater is led into a basin and allowed to stand, this material will drop out. Before the advent of efficient treatment methods, the nation's health depended completely on this storage practice for improving the quality of water to the point at which it became safe. Long storage greatly reduces turbidity and some of the nastier bugs, such as the bacteria of intestinal origin, typhoid and other waterborne diseases disappear. To some extent this seems to be due simply to sedimentation but there is also some bactericidal action brought about through the ultraviolet radiation from the sun. The fact that bacteria counts are usually lower in the surface layers of reservoirs points to this.

Prolonged storage is not without some disadvantage, however, the major one being the growth of algae, which increases the difficulties of treatment. The algal 'blooms' characteristic of excesses of plant nutrients in the water create a seasonal problem which has grown in magnitude in recent years. The main culprits are the high levels of nitrate and phosphate in the water and opinions differ about whether agriculture or sewage effluent is to blame.

The remaining particles which have not settled out within a few days are removed by flocculation using coagulating chemicals. The water then goes into slow sand filters where many of the impurities are left behind in the pores or on the surfaces of the grains. Sandbeds have been used since the earlyyears of the last century. They

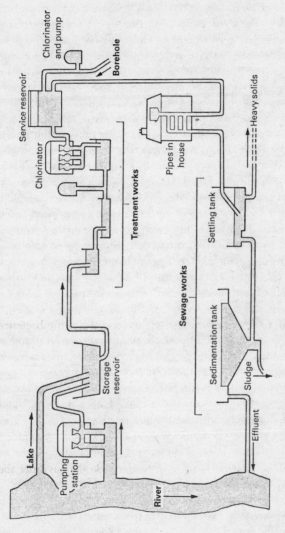

Figure 15 Treatment cycle for public water supply.

are extremely efficient in purifying the water bacteriologically as well as cleaning it physically, and indeed the whole of London's surface water supplies are still treated in this way today.

Water filters down through two to three feet of sand laid over a bed of fine gravel, beneath which are collecting pipes. The water floods the bed completely (as opposed to trickling over the surface as in sewage farm filters) and is left to filter under gravity. As the suspended matter in the water is deposited on the surface of the sand grains so the filtration rate slows up. This is counteracted by increasing the head of water up to the point when the rate is so slow that the sand must be cleaned. If some prefiltration system is used, the sandbeds can last up to several months between cleanings, although intervals as short as ten days are not uncommon. Quite how they work is not clear. It is certainly not just a simple straining process, for complex microbiological actions are known to play their part. During the first days of operation the upper layers of sand become coated with reddish-brown deposits of partly decomposed matter and particles of iron, manganese, aluminium and silica. This coating tends to absorb extra organic matter passing through in a colloidal state. After a while a film of algae, bacteria and protozoa establishes itself and the whole lot together then acts as a very fine mesh. Below this mat is a zone where the growing plant life (the algae) breaks down organic matter, decomposes the plankton and uses up the available nutrients (nitrates, phosphates and CO_2) releasing oxygen in their place. Below this region the bacteria multiply in vast numbers and complete the breakdown of the remaining organic matter. They also destroy themselves in time as food and oxygen are used up so that what comes out at the bottom is clean drinking water containing very little extraneous matter.

Any potentially dangerous organisms still left in the water are dealt with by disinfection. The usual agent is chlorine which is cheap, reliable and fairly easy to handle, although ozone, iodine and exposure to ultraviolet rays are sometimes used. How the chlorine kills the bacteria is another curious unknown. The general belief is that the chlorine compounds formed in the water interfere with certain enzymes in the bacteria cells; it seems unlikely that it is a straightforward oxidation process because the quantities that suffice to disinfect the water completely are much too small.

We take the safety of water so much for granted that it is salutary to remember that as recently as 1904 deaths from a typhoid epidemic in Lincoln were traced to bad water. The drastic emergency measures taken to curb the spread of the disease, known to have affected at least fifteen hundred people, included chlorinating the water, the first time this had been done in Britain.

At some stage in the process water is aerated both to release gases in solution (which improves taste and odour) and to dissolve as much oxygen as possible, which can then oxygenate harmful substances still present. Decaying vegetation can give a musty or fishy odour or taste to water. Water left standing in pipes for some time overnight in a large centrally heated office building, for instance, often causes taste problems. Such ideal conditions for the growth of microorganisms may mean that the first water drawn off in the morning has a decidedly nasty taste. Another problem arises with minute traces of phenols left in the water, which in the presence of chlorine added during disinfection can produce the quite awful taste of chlorphenol. Amazingly, as little as one part in 500 million can be detected, so powerful is the taste. Phenols get into the water supply either as a component of wastewater from industrial processes or even through the picking up of tarry substances from the roads; rainwater washing down into the gutters from recently repaired roads can eventually end up somewhere in a storage reservoir, still carrying traces of phenols. It is a silly anomaly in water administration that surface water from roofs and yards is the responsibility of the water authorities but not water draining from roads, which is the province of the highway authorities. Severe pollution may result from spillage when tankers are involved in road accidents, especially if salvage work is delayed for any reason.

Chlorine itself does not have a pronounced taste except in very large doses. One way to overcome taste problems is first to overchlorinate to make sure every scrap of organic matter has gone and then to dechlorinate with sulphur dioxide. The idea of chemical treatment for water is abhorrent to some, who favour ozone treatment as being a more 'natural' method of disinfection. The domestic filters fitted to taps in individual households usually rely on activated charcoal, which is highly efficient at removing complex organic molecules. Often complaints about the taste of water are solved simply by flushing out old mains, where rust discolours the water and adds its own distinctive flavour.

Water authorities have to provide temporary storage or service reservoirs at strategic points in the distribution network to overcome the problem of fluctuating demand. There is also the problem of dealing with failures in the trunkline. Even the best repair gangs may need several hours to locate and patch up leaks, especially if the fault is noticed at night. The recommendation is for supply authorities to have service storage for a minimum of twenty-four hours supply. Unfortunately, lack of money means that in many cases this is just not available. To be more effective, the service storage should be as near as possible to the main demand areas, and sited on high ground or in a water tower to minimize pressure requirements.

The water in this type of storage is very clean, having been made ready for drinking at great trouble and expense. Not surprisingly it is guarded with extra care against pollution. Storage tanks are roofed over to prevent the attention of seagulls or pigeons, which after feeding at sewage farms have a bad habit of washing themselves in any convenient open water. The unwanted attention of small children has caused many a headache too; there was a case reported recently of the enforced shutdown of a town's water supply when an observant water engineer spotted what he thought were specks of detergent on the water and which turned out to be rat poison deposited by a misguided junior citizen.

From the service reservoirs the water enters the mains where it is pushed round under pressure, the mains pressure which is obvious when you turn on the tap. This pressure can be boosted at key points when necessary to meet demands at times when the drawoff is high. It can also be reduced as a crude way of saving water during dry periods, since this minimizes the loss through seepage from defective pipes. In many rural areas these mains pipes are still only the original two inches in diameter. This means that some dry weather restrictions are simply because the demand is such that the pipes are too small to maintain the required pressure. The pipes which convey the water from the distribution mains to individual houses are called service pipes. They are half an inch in diameter and can be made of lead, copper, wrought iron, steel or plastic.

4 Users and Consumers:
Matching Supply to Demand

No one would pretend that the water authorities have an easy job. Future supply projections must be based on the current demand and supply situations, figures for which are scant and unreliable. Population figures obtained by a national census take a long time to be produced, and are thus probably out of date when they arrive; moreover the boundaries used for the census do not coincide with those of either current or past water supply authorities. Further, towns with any kind of tourist attractions have very fluctuating demands – a hosepipe ban had to be placed on parts of Devon in the wet August of 1977 simply because the influx of holidaymakers exhausted local supplies. Even days of the week, such as Monday washday, cause fluctuations.

The first authoritative figures on future national demand were those produced by the Department of the Environment's Central Water Planning Unit (now disbanded). In 1969, according to the Unit, demand for public water supplies was increasing by seven litres per head each year. This was based on forecasts made in 1965 of the expected future population of England and Wales, which projected a total of sixty-six million inhabitants in the year 2001. By 1973 the population forecast had been lowered to fifty-six million by 2001 and the forecast increase of per capita demand slackened off to five litres per head a day. Now the population likely at the close of the century is thought to be some fifty-two million for England and Wales, making some of the more ambitious water resource schemes put forward in recent years unnecessary.

Actual physiological needs are just three litres a day for the average active person in temperate climates – a very small amount indeed compared to the gross weight of the body. But as consumers each of us currently accounts for over 300 litres daily (1975 figures), a figure still increasing as more labour-saving, water-intensive appliances come into use. Even before the 1975–6 drought proved their point, many water undertakings were saying at the beginning of the decade that they could not match supply to demand under the stress of a dry summer. This unease is claimed to be behind the drastic shake-up of the water industry which took place in 1973.

The service the public gets from its water industry is pretty good in this country: statistics giving the percentage of the population with piped water and connected to mains sewerage, the constant wholesomeness of mains water, and the slow but sure improvement in the quality of our rivers, add up to a better record than any other nation. This is of course highly satisfactory but costs a lot of money. The capital financing of the ten Regional Water Authorities serving England and Wales totals well over a thousand million pounds each year.★ The most recent figures available (1982–3) show a total revenue expenditure by this same group of £2,075 million, of which slightly over half relates to water conservation, distribution and supply, and the rest is concerned with sewage collection, treatment and disposal.

As well as domestic water rates (based on the rateable value of the building), there is a considerable income arising from the charges made to industrial users who have metered supplies. These consumers, numbering about 650,000, are charged per thousand gallons (4·55 cubic metres)† at varying prices related partly to the cost of the installation and partly to the volume used but usually subject to certain

Table 1   Percentage Costs of Water Supply

Supply (catchment areas, reservoirs and boreholes)	15
Treatment	18
Transmission to centres of consumption	15
Distribution	27
Rates	10
Management and general	15

★ £1,108 million in 1980–1.

† The water industry is trying hard to convert uniformly to metric units but there are occasions when the conversion from gallons to litres (or cubic metres as appropriate) is unwieldy. Where this situation arises, as in the instance above, the original units have been left since changing to metric does nothing to aid the reader's comprehension.

minimum charges. The costs rise every year, even more sharply than domestic rates; the 1977 price of 49p per 1,000 gallons had become 92p per 1,000 gallons in 1982 – virtually doubled in just five years. These metred supplies account for about 30 per cent of the water supplied in England and Wales, and of this volume about 40 per cent is left untreated and supplied to those industries who do not need clean water.

Since much of the money for water supplies is collected as a tax rather than from the sale of a commodity like other public utilities, it is not surprising to find the system has some anachronisms. Domestic supplies provide revenue through water rates which at present bear no relation to the cost of installing or maintaining the supply, being based on the value of the property concerned. Private households supply 82 per cent of the income from water rates. The remaining 18 per cent is levied on supplies to commercial properties (even though these use only about 6 per cent of the water supplied, 94 per cent being used for domestic purposes in houses, garden watering and vehicle washing).

Table 2 shows some interesting trends in water consumption. A few years ago industry was the biggest user but this is no longer true (see Figure 16). However, industrial water requirements are still massive even though the water is used only temporarily, about half the firms returning it directly into the sewerage systems

Table 2   Water Abstraction

	1975 (million litres/day)	percentage of total	1981 (million litres/day)	percentage of total
Public water supply	15,288	40	16,200	50·5
Direct industrial abstraction	8,790	23	5,400	16·8
CEGB cooling water	14,141	37	10,500	32·7
Total water abstracted	38,219	100	32,100	100

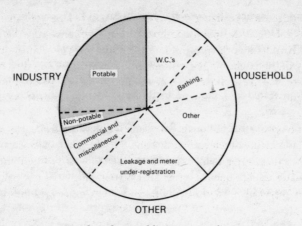

Figure 16 Categories of use from public water supplies.

or into the nearest watercourse and the rest discharging waste directly into estuaries or out to sea. Industry has several different uses for water – the most common is for heat exchange or coolant and it is also used as a solvent or as a transport agent, as a washing agent and for raising steam. Yet it is comparatively rare for water to be actually 'consumed' in the production process. In all, only about 5 per cent of the industrial demand for water is lost to the water industry through incorporation into manufactured products, or disappears as steam into the atmosphere.

Traditional figures relating to demand in various processing industries have recently been shown to be much too high. A few years ago the planners within the water industry used to talk soberly of the 200 litres needed to produce just one pint of beer or the 200,000 litres for one motor car tyre. The shortages of the last few years, however, led inquiring journalists to probe into various industrial processes and the revised figures now quoted come down to 9 litres for a pint of beer and 68 litres for a tyre. Nevertheless, the volumes involved are still large and cause sufficient headaches in many firms. For instance, a large paper mill can use more water in one day than a town of fifty thousand inhabitants.

Before the 1976 drought every vehicle marketed by British Leyland included £1 in its price to cover the costs of the water needed during its manufacture. Realizing that water must cost at least 50p per 1,000 gallons (or over 10p per 1,000 litres) from 1978 onwards, the firm took a hard look at the processes where water was being squandered, mainly the body cleaning operations before painting. Costs then came down to 30p per vehicle since economies had been made, reputed to be equal to a £1 million saving on water bills over the next three years.

Not only volume but quality of water is crucial for some processes. The manufacture of television tubes and transistors, for instance, needs much cleaner water than, say, the manufacture of synthetic fibres. And water used in quenching or for gas scrubbing need not be clean at all. Conversely, water for boiler feed, working at pressures up to

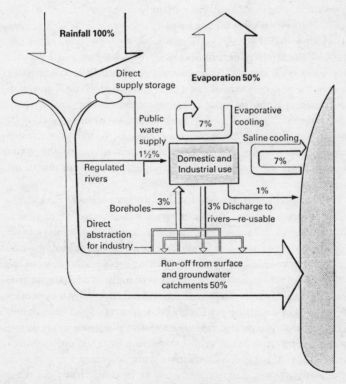

Figure 17 Water balance for England and Wales.

thirty-five atmospheres, not only has to be of very high quality but also needs special treatment to adjust its alkalinity. Although most scale-forming salts are taken out, it is sensible to leave the water slightly scale-forming so that a protective coating is built up on metal surfaces which would otherwise corrode. Sometimes it is more convenient to make sure that the process equipment used suits the chemistry of the water available than to install expensive treatment plant. Heat exchangers using estuary water, for example, need to be made of materials able to withstand saltwater corrosion.

Direct abstraction of riverwater for industrial use is declining, being offset by a corresponding increase in demand for mains water with its guaranteed minimum quality. This could simply be because industrial processes are getting more complicated, a natural reflection of the increasing sophistication of manufactured goods.

The largest single user of water is the Central Electricity Generating Board (CEGB). Water is the working fluid in the heat cycle of steam turbo-generators, which produce up to 98 per cent of electricity in Britain. Where water is plentiful, as when power stations are sited on the banks of a river or estuary, water is abstracted directly for passing into the cooling system. It then returns to the river some $11°C$ warmer. Tower coolers are used where water supplies are limited. Here all the water from the condensers goes through cooling towers before returning to a nearby watercourse such as a river or canal and is then usually only some $6°C$ above the natural water temperature.

Many power stations have a combination of both types of cooling. The spectacular plumes of water vapour issuing from the tops of cooling towers, although undoubtedly a loss to the system, perhaps surprisingly account for only about 9 per cent of the water within the power station cycle. Quotation of average quantities used is not very meaningful because of the seasonal changes in demand for electricity and the daily cycles which produce midday loads and a falling off towards midnight; 31,000 million tonnes (18,700 million gallons a day) is the figure quoted for 1982, of which 11,800 million gallons a day was provided by recycling water in power stations and 5,300 million gallons a day by abstraction from lower estuaries and the sea, leaving 1,600 million gallons a day to be provided by the water authorities.

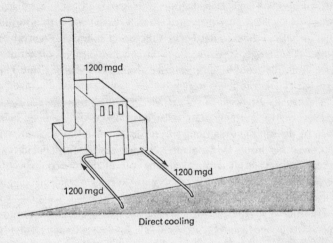

Direct cooling

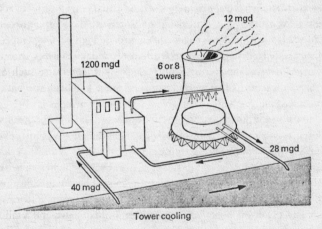

Tower cooling

Figure 18 Cooling water cycle in power stations (mgd = million gallons/day).

There are signs that demands may diminish, since less cooling water is needed with improved thermal efficiency. Also the increasing use of cooling towers instead of direct abstraction allows greater scope for recycling. However there may then be problems with unwanted algal growth in the pipe networks if the water contains excess organic matter. The danger is that if chemicals are added to kill off the algae there could be trouble with poisoning of wild life when this water is released back into the watercourse.

As virtually any kind of water will do for cooling, there are good reasons for siting power stations at estuaries or on the coast, since there are no limits to the amount of seawater available. Unfortunately, though, other limits then operate, because electricity demand tends to be more concentrated inland and the costs of cheaper cooling water have to be balanced against expensive and unsightly transmission lines marching across the countryside.

Traditionally, anyone owning land by a river could use as much riverwater as he wanted for agricultural purposes providing only that any surplus abstracted was allowed to drain back to the river. Quite often such riparian land carried permitted abstraction rights for other uses too. With the passing of the 1963 Water Act, which set up river authorities to control resources more tightly, industry gave up its common law rights in the national interest for the better management of water. In turn, the water authorities granted licences to industries for the abstraction of needed water, and were required to do their part in providing adequate supply and proper treatment facilities for the resulting effluent entering the sewerage systems. The river authorities were allowed to charge for licences as a way of raising money to pay for resource activities.

Apart from firms setting up factories near estuaries when they only need water for cooling and can therefore accept a certain saline content, there is no obvious siting of industries in relation to water costs. Particular types of water can be important, however. Historically the textile industries grew up where there was access to soft upland water, while the brewers and the paper makers looked for hard water. Modern technology and the economics of construction and transport now often make it more sensible to operate large, centralized plant and accept the cost of special treatment processes. One of the large brewing combines even goes so far as to deionize its water intake and then dose it up with variable amounts of appropriate salts to re-create water similar in taste to those of the different districts from which its component breweries have been transferred.

There appears to be a trend towards direct groundwater abstraction in places lucky enough to have such resources. Groundwater chemistry is extremely stable, which permits a certain amount of standardization in the deionizing or demineralizing that has to go on when the water is purified for high technology applications.

An increasingly heavy burden on many industries is the cost of effluent treatment and disposal. Public opinion and official pressures have stopped many of the abuses of natural watercourses. There are still some minor rivers in the heavily industrialized regions which are described as no better than open sewers but matters are slowly improving. It is now an admitted principle that effluent treatment is part of production costs. But while it is accepted that 'the polluter pays', there remains the vexed question of where the effluent treatment should take place. The view of the employers' organization, the Confederation of British Industry, is that while it may best be done at the factory it is sometimes better left to the sewerage works and that no standardization is feasible. This attitude leaves loopholes for the worst offender, and the water authorities push hard for improvement in effluent treatment before any wastewater leaves the factory premises.

With industry forced to pay both for its intake water and its effluent, one may ask what effect such financial constraints are likely to have on future projections of demand for water. Initially, there will probably be little change; any cutback in intake is likely to make effluent more concentrated and more costly to treat, thus negating any savings. In the long term, such pressure must surely affect the pace at which effluent treatment techniques improve and ways are found to recycle water more efficiently within plant. The Royal Commission on Environmental Pollution, which might be said to voice the general public's attitude to despoliation of the countryside, wants to see all rivers become salmon rivers again by the end of the century. Is it worth the cost, asks industry?

Ignoring for the moment the general responsibility we all share as fellow citizens for the protection of our environment, there is little positive incentive for firms to improve the quality of their effluent.

There is at least a case for some kind of rebate if industrial water leaves the premises at or above a certain minimum quality. Better still, rather than continue to tackle each area's industrial effluent problems in a piecemeal fashion, why cannot there be a unifying strategy? Is there no chance for the kind of overview that would plan the siting of new development near conurbations in such a way that water in domestic sewers could be reused by local firms? This would seem to be a far safer way of coping with water demand than the conventional method of having to treat all sewage, industrial and domestic alike, to the same high standards necessary for water of potable quality. Where firms are using clean water abstracted from deep wells, there must be scope for providing alternative, not-so-pure water (possibly from domestic waste) and so releasing the natural groundwater for use in the public supply. A further step would be the siting together of industries whose effluents are such that the noxious contents go some way to cancelling each other out.

Meanwhile, however, although a few industries are where they are because of some aspect of their water needs, the development of areas with high rates of unemployment is more likely to influence planning policies, both now and in the foreseeable future. Consequently current cutbacks in the allocation of funds for capital investment in mains supplies or sewerage installations put the water authorities in an unfavourable light when planning applications for new development are refused.

Agriculture is one of the largest industries in this country and a correspondingly lavish user of water. Figures for abstraction licences, mostly for irrigation, do not of course account for the water coming out of the mains supply or the industry's use of the prime resource itself, the raw untreated rainfall. As in most other industries water is needed for washing, a demand which is increasing with more and more vegetables being sold ready cleaned in shrink-wrap packaging through supermarket outlets. Animals too are thirsty creatures, a cow in milk accounting for some thirty gallons a day (half of which she drinks, the other half being needed for milk cooling and washing dairy equipment) while pigs use three gallons a day and sheep and lambs about a gallon and a half.

When it comes to crop production, however, water really is consumed and not 'borrowed' for cooling or whatever as in most industries. The rate of use of water in any particular locality is probably more affected by temperature than by any other factor. This is because transpiration, the process of water movement and evaporation from leaf surfaces, proceeds at a faster rate the higher the temperature. Transpiration loss is complicated by the fact that it will also be greater the larger the area of leaf surface, a factor related to plant maturity. Thus the heaviest demands will come towards the end of the growing season, just when the soil reserves are at their lowest and rainfall is erratic or non-existent. Losses also happen more quickly if the air round plants is moving.

Experiments have shown that when water uptake is severely limited the physiological processes that promote growth within plants stop as much as two days before there are any obvious signs of wilting. The plants stop growing because, although cell division goes on, the new cells do not extend to their full potential through lack of water to fill the cell vacuole. When water does become available again, the small leaves and stems produced during high moisture stress never reach their full size and such stunted plants seldom catch up with others grown without these checks. Farmers and growers, being in business to maximize production from the land, have to weigh carefully the undoubted extra yield from crops irrigated during dry periods against the heavy installation and abstraction costs incurred. Even when the cost is justified, there is seldom any leeway for treatment plant. Instead the type of crop grown is chosen to suit the water supply and to overcome local quality differences, except in the Channel Islands where the high value tomato crop supports a desalination plant for use in water shortage emergencies.

The abnormally dry summers of 1975 and 1976 resulted in a flood of extra spray irrigation licence applications in the dry eastern parts of the country where the farmers suffered most. The Anglian Water Authority, who are responsible for water supplies in this area, had over six hundred licence applications in the twelve-month period following the drought, their normal annual quota being between forty and fifty. This has caused some consternation because it is not yet clear whether this is just panic reaction to a couple of very dry years or really does reflect a changing emphasis in water demand for farming. It has been authoritatively said that there is scope for a ten-fold increase in irrigation over this region, providing the water

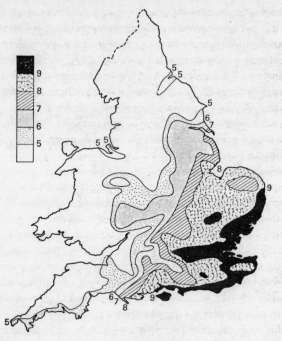

Figure 19 General frequency of irrigation need (years in ten).

is available. Such a big step would of course make a significant contribution to the nation's food production. It may be said that the theoretical improvements in yield from judicious watering, advocated for years by agricultural research workers, are being taken seriously at last. Several factors now make this possible, such as developments in agricultural machinery, farm management and not least in food prices. The machine technology input is important because the new generation of 'rainguns' cut out much of the labour problems of older-style equipment; extra labour costs on top of capital for equipment used to absorb all the extra income from bigger yields. Management education is important too because irrigation is a tricky business which has to be done right to make it pay. Finally there is plain economics. Farmers are under pressure to increase production, prices have increased in real terms, increasing the profit from marginal increases in yield, and EEC membership means that every year they must produce at least average yields. Previously a poor year at home pushed up the prices for those crops in scarce supply; now all produce is in market competition with crops from the rest of Europe.

Perfect irrigation practice is very difficult to achieve. Both too much and too little water are extremely harmful to the crop. Too little not only negates potential yield but, by filling only the upper pore spaces of the soil, encourages the roots to develop too near the surface where they shrivel up during following dry periods. Traditionally it was assumed that growing plants where water is in short supply in the upper soil layers is not harmful because it encourages deep rooting. Newer thinking suggests that this argument is not valid, that deep rooting is a survival exercise and does little for productivity. More seriously unirrigated crops consume their own food reserves to stay alive in dry conditions, thereby depressing the quality of yield.

On the other hand, over-irrigation, especially on poorly drained soils, keeps out the air which plant roots need. It also stops the decomposition of organic matter, vital for the soil's supply of nutrients; excessive watering will in time leach out the valuable constituents of the soil. The ultimate aim is always to supply just sufficient to ensure that water is not a limiting factor in growth. In quantitative terms this means keeping the top 300 millimetres of the soil at 50–80 per cent of field capacity.

Crops grown in intensive systems such as market gardens or glasshouses can exploit different kinds of permanent system. Crops grown in the open are usually spray irrigated, often from mobile equipment, the water supply coming either from the mains where available or from private sources such as streams or boreholes. The amount of water required is enormous. Crops need approximately 25 millimetres of rainfall every eight to ten days during dry summer periods: to supply that amount of water over just one hectare needs a volume of water equivalent to that contained in two or three fuel tankers or that which flows out of a tap left running continuously for some ten days. The strain that this sort of demand puts on the country's water resources is such that every year there are parts of the country where the demand exceeds the volume of the water flowing in the rivers of that area.

A water authority licence is required before water can be legally abstracted from either surface or underground sources for spray irrigation unless there are special exception orders available for that area. Fees are charged on the granting of licences which stipulate the amount of water to be abstracted and the periods when it may be used. Annual charges are made with supplementary amounts for varying quantities. The licensee thus has a 'protected right' to the water he needs, which is supposed to compensate for his giving up the common law rights he may have enjoyed as a riparian land owner. There are severe limitations in practice. In periods of excessively dry weather, Drought Orders can prohibit all spray irrigation operations. The increasing demand for water for all purposes means that less and less water is available during the summer for new or increased irrigation, and hence more is being spent on the construction of reservoir storage on individual farms.

The majority of crops grown in the open experience soil moisture deficits in most years. A few short dry spells may go by unrecognized or underestimated but can still reduce yields. How far it is economically sound to correct these deficits depends on their frequency and the value of the crop – it is probably worthwhile with root crops such as new potatoes but not for cereals or pasture. Even in the case of pasture, though, the changing practices in farming may make it economic sense to husband grassland to the extent that it will support very high stocking yields for dairy herds; herbage provides half the water intake for grazing animals. The number of years when irrigation pays off depends not only on the crop but also on the weather patterns and to a lesser extent on the soil type. Those unfortunate enough to have open, free-draining sandy soils may find themselves irrigating more frequently than their neighbours because their particular patch has little soil reservoir to sustain growth.

Agriculturalists and meteorologists working together over the years have devised irrigation schedules applicable to each region and for all types of crops. Even knowing roughly how much water will be needed, there is still the problem of when to apply it. It is no good waiting until the plants show obvious signs of wilting – the physiological damage will have been done by then. The appropriate information is published weekly in the MORECS Bulletins issued by the Meteorological Office, showing the soil moisture deficit in each area. They are based on previous rainfall input and the potential transpiration loss calculated from climatic variables. Because rain may fall immediately after irrigation, which wastes water and possibly leaches out valuable nutrients, it is common practice to compromise and to satisfy only part of the water demand.

Permanent irrigation equipment is only likely to be used with high-value cash crops. In some cases, however, it is possible for the installation to help pay for itself in other ways, such as frost protection, so important in fruit growing. Two approaches are possible. The first is to irrigate the soil not long before a night frost is likely. Wet and compact soil is a better conductor of heat than dry and loose soil. Irrigation both wets and compacts the soil and leads to greater heat absorption on a warm day and greater upward transfer of heat from the soil to the air during a clear cold night. Air above wet bare soil can be $1°C$ warmer than above dry bare soil, a temperature difference vital to valuable low growing crops such as strawberries. Secondly, continuous sprinkling is used to protect fruit tree blossom and depends on the transfer of heat from the water, mainly by the latent heat of freezing of water as it turns to ice. Success occurs only if there is a film of water always present to be turned into ice.

With rising land prices, labour shortages and all the other troubles besetting modern agriculture, there is a tendency towards all-out maximization of the pipe network. Thus the equipment is used not only for irrigation and frost protection but also to dispense liquid fertilizers, pesticides and even to raise the humidity on hot days to keep the leaf pores open so that maximum crop growth is kept up.

Every summer weekend there are more people messing about in boats than there are spectators at professional football matches on an average winter weekend. In all, it is estimated that for some $5\frac{3}{4}$ million people in Britain water-based leisure activities are an integral part of their lives. And such a classification still leaves out those with fringe interests in water such as campers, bird watchers and ramblers. At present England and Wales have over 80,000 hectares of water suitable for recreation with an estimated further 18,000 hectares of new reservoir facilities and 14,000 hectares of gravel pits likely to be available by the year 2000. Despite these increases, the growth in leisure pursuits generally may mean there will still be a shortage of facilities by the end of the century.

The new powers given to the ten regional water authorities by the Water Act of 1973 allow considerable scope for managing inland waterways in a fashion that improves their amenity value. In fact, the Act requires that the best use be made of rivers, canals and reservoirs for the benefit of the public's recreational needs in the widest possible sense. There was originally a Water Space Amenity Commission set up as an offshoot of the National Water Council (also now defunct) to review progress in the development of all forms of water amenity, not just the water space controlled by the water authorities (about 50 per cent of the total). The growing concern for this aspect of our water heritage is reflected in the way that new reservoir schemes are designed with recreational use in mind. Thus the new Queen Mother Reservoir near Heathrow Airport opened in July 1976 is the first of London's thirteen bankside reservoirs to have a specially created 'beach' or boat park and club house to cater for the sailing fraternity, and to be stocked with 100,000 young trout for fishing. And a great chunk of the cost of the controversial Kielder Water reservoir related to the amenity and recreational facilities provided.

We are lucky in having a fairly even distribution of rivers throughout the land, although there are some that are none too savoury for recreational pursuits. The official policy of the Department of the Environment is to continue the fight to improve the quality of all our rivers to the extent that they will be able to support at least some species of fish. This means an increasing burden on the effluent treatment processes, whether they are at the factory or at the local sewage works. Either way, the cost is still prohibitive and any improvement is bound to be slow. Meanwhile the water authorities earmark about £1 million per annum for the support of fisheries. Half of this money they recover by charging for fishing licences and rents and half is diverted from the local authorities. There are currently about a million people whose sport is angling for coarse fish, the native non-migratory fish such as roach, dace, bass, pike and eel which populate many of our rivers. Fishing for trout or salmon is restricted to fast-flowing very clean streams, usually found in unspoilt rural areas, or nowadays in specially stocked reservoirs. Numbers taking part are kept down by the cost of fishing rights to the best salmon or trout streams. Nevertheless there are now many syndicates operating who are prepared to pay large sums and travel widely for their sport. Angling ranks as the most popular of all water-based sports after swimming.

While the more active pursuits like water skiing need fairly large expanses of water such as lakes or reservoirs (10–15 hectares being regarded as the minimum space necessary for skiing) there are also a great many people who find satisfaction in exploring the canal network of the country. Thanks to the enthusiasm of the various industrial archaeological groups and conservation societies, much of the network has been opened up once more for the enjoyment of thousands. But although the voluntary societies do a lot to improve disused canals there is still a hefty burden on the state for the maintenance and operation of many miles of inland waterways, a large proportion of which are still used commercially. The annual expenditure by the British Waterways Board, the authority responsible for the canals before it was merged with the National Water Council, was £5 million in 1977. About half this amount was recovered by tolls, rents and charges for various amenity uses, and also by selling some of the water supplies: the remainder came from central government grants. The water sold to industry is of course returned after use. The quality of this water can be pretty poor, but as canals often go right through the centre of older industrial towns they are a very important, and in some areas the biggest single, source of cooling water for local industry. The total water assets of the canal network have been estimated at between 130 and 180 million litres (30–40 million gallons) of water, and the industrial exploitation of this resource brings in over £500,000 a year.

Even on the conservative estimate of 3,000 kilometres of canal, mostly constructed during the eighteenth and nineteenth centuries, the canals of Britain are an impressive monument to past civil engineers. So much thought went into their planning and operation – for example, the skilful construction of the networks so that upland feeder reservoirs and a minimal number of intake points would keep the levels stable by gravitational flow of the water for very long distances. Inevitably many people still press for the canals to be considered an integral part of the nation's transport system. Whatever their navigational usefulness in the future, there is no doubt that water engineers have often considered their place in a national water grid. So far, the inter-regional coordination necessary for large scale water transfers has not been very evident, but the organizational changes of recent years, designed to manage water as a national resource, may change the situation. Many are worried about the future amenity value of the canals, with the possibility that the water authorities will reduce them to the status of drainage and water supply conduits only. There is the inescapable fact that the backlog of maintenance charges is in the region of £60 million, a bill that no organization will pick up lightly.

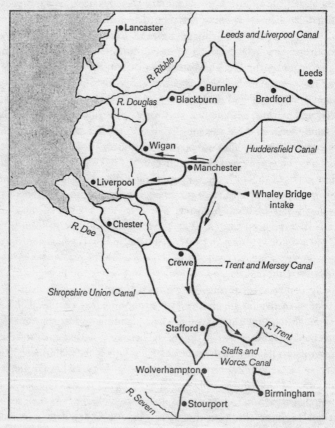

Figure 20 Potential distribution of water from the Whaley Bridge intake via the canal system of north-west England.

5 *Water Out of Control*

Most commodities have their share of production, operation or distribution problems. Water is no exception and has the added complication that the production process is totally outside the engineer's control. Embarrassing shortages or over-production bear absolutely no relation to market forces.

Successive Water Acts have laid down that it is the responsibility of water authorities to provide adequate supplies of wholesome water at minimal cost. And this is of course exactly what happens in practice for the vast majority of the time. Water, being the universal, cheap, freely available commodity that it is in this country, is hardly ever mentioned when counting the cost of maintaining a reasonable standard of living.

Providing enough water, whether for drinking or for industry, is just one side of things. A decent standard of living also means not letting excess water get out of hand. A short succession of bleak wet winter days soon turns unmetalled roads and paths into muddy quagmires and fills rivers to the top of their banks. From that point on, flooding happens all too easily if the weather stays against us.

River channels have been formed over the ages and, left to themselves, will just accommodate the maximum flows of average wet seasons. A deviation in the rainfall pattern which increases the runoff from the land inundates the area along the riverbank, known as the floodplain. The random variability of the weather means that floodplains are likely to be covered at least once every four or five years.

There is no doubt that such elementary environmental interactions were recognized by our forebears, who deliberately chose sites for villages to avoid floods. Even the City of London, largely on the same site as the early Roman settlement of Londinium, is pretty well floodproof. We can hardly blame our ancestors for lacking the foresight to see how their small towns would expand from the dry terraces to the neighbouring floodplains because of the pressures of modern living.

Another feature of urban development which aggravates flooding is the tendency to encroach on the river channel itself. Wharves, embankments, the piers of bridges, all tend to constrict and impede the river so that flood levels are higher than if it were left in its natural state. The banking and walls which now line the Thames where it passes through London have increased the yearly highest water levels by over three feet in the last hundred and fifty years.

There are two sorts of floods. Firstly, there is what is called 'flash flooding' when sudden heavy rain falls on impermeable surfaces and cannot drain away fast enough. The worst hit are areas such as town parks with battered playing fields whose surfaces are iron-hard, or parts of towns where the planners have been over-zealous in their use of concrete paving. Here, although there may be plenty of drains, the suddenness and intensity of some freak storms produce too great a volume of water to get down the gutters, and it takes a few hours for excess water to clear. Low-lying fields, especially the water meadows on the banks of rivers, often have water lying in them after prolonged wet periods, for the soil is so saturated with water that it can absorb no more. These types of shortlived flood have considerable nuisance value and can cause lost agricultural production as well as inconvenience.

The second and more serious type of flooding happens when a river overtops its banks because too much water is draining in from its catchment area. This not only wreaks greater havoc but can be a killer on occasions. Of course a lot can be done through the general management of a river to avert serious flooding without having to build special relief channels. It is standard practice on major rivers like the Thames, where weirs and locks allow tight control of the flow, to juggle with the excess water. It is either allowed to overtop the banks along certain stretches, since flooded fields are less of a hazard than flooded villages further downstream, or diverted into bankside storage reservoirs. Although there are now very few 'natural' rivers left, with dredging, reinforced banks and complex sluices all very much in evidence, it is nevertheless a fair tribute to the river managers that widescale floods like those of the immediate post-war period have not been seen since.

Flood damage is insidious: there are not only the losses which can be evaluated in money terms but also the distress factors, ranging from breakdown in communications to health hazards. Currently, some £65 million is spent on flood alleviation each year. This represents about 6 per cent of the total expenditure of the water authorities, who confine their activities to the principal river channels and other watercourses found in urban settings. Land drainage, another form of flood alleviation, is the province of the Ministry of Agriculture. The money for floodworks comes either from loans serviced through the rates or grant-aid from the Ministry of Agriculture or as direct contributions from local authorities, other public bodies or private organizations who stand to benefit from specific schemes. Assessing likely flood losses is a vital first step in any proposal for relief. The benefits from a good alleviation scheme are obviously given by the difference between the damage occurring without the scheme and what will happen with it. So we have first to know how much damage to expect and also how often it may happen. It is clearly good sense to spend say £50,000 to avert £20,000 of damage occurring every year but not so sensible if that amount of damage happens only once in every hundred years.

Such cost-accounting may not apply in every case. Public money is often spent in more altruistic fashion with benefits that may not be so obviously financial. Indeed, to make a rather sweeping generalization, economic evaluations are done as an appendage to most flood alleviation design processes rather than as integral parts of them – to the annoyance of more farsighted insurance brokers. This is probably as it should be, with the prevailing attitude quite rightly being that it is fairer to put in hand projects that minimize the flood risks to individuals even though they may on balance be less beneficial to the community than other possible ones. Unfortunately there are no statutory powers to insist that such generalized requirements are met, and cases where road and building development have aggravated waterlogged conditions or even caused actual flooding can be quoted virtually every year. The sad fact is that care taken to guard against all eventualities in new developments, such as infilling to raise the floor level in factories or houses built on known floodplains, while it protects these new buildings will almost always increase flood levels elsewhere because it will have stopped the floodwater from taking its normal overflow pathways.

It is not always damage to buildings that costs most money. Another feature to consider is the cost of the disruption to transport through reduced speeds or lengthy detours to avoid flooded roads. The following table is based on traffic census figures for 1969 when the average daily flow on trunk roads was approximately nine thousand vehicles. Needless to say, there are loading factors to be used to adjust the figures for today's increased volume of traffic and time valuations.

Table 3   Cost of One Hour Delay Imposed on Traffic

Category of vehicle	Proportion of total vehicles	Number of vehicles	Rate £/hr	Cost £
Car	78%	7000	0·93*	6500
Goods	20%	1800	0·66**	1200
Bus	2%	200	4·08	800
			Total cost	8500

*Mean of working and leisure rates
**Mean of rates for heavy and light goods vehicles

Much harder to assess are the long-term benefits from improving drainage to increase the productivity of land which previously had been inundated one or more times a year. Not only is damage to crops avoided but it may be possible to switch to more intensive forms of agriculture. Not surprisingly, competition for Ministry grants is very keen.

On the premise that prevention is better than cure, some means of flood prevention is an integral part of all new road and bridge design; an estimated 10 per cent of motorway costs are directly related to drainage. Also in many cases population pressure has forced development in areas known to be prone to flooding, so that each year many existing high-risk highways, particularly in urban areas, are the subject of flood relief schemes. Wherever possible these have practical spinoff benefits. New culverts or embankments are built to channel the water usefully, either to top up local storage reservoirs or to create a recreational bonus in the form of temporary boating pools in town parks, as with Netteswell Pond in Harlow New Town. There is some rough justice in this since most alleviation schemes will be to the detriment of that most popular pastime for kids and grownups alike, namely fishing. What is more, this will be a permanent effect whether or not a flood actually happens. This is because fish thrive in meandering, slow-moving waters with stony beds and rough over-grown banks, all features which are anathema to the drainage engineer aiming for straight, smooth channels to clear water as quickly as possible.

This is the big trouble with flood relief. Many potential solutions pose almost as many environmental problems as they solve. Reservoirs and washlands (i.e. areas deliberately allowed to flood) use up valuable land in a non-productive way; relief culverts fill with silt; enlarged channels probably have only very shallow flows in dry weather, exposing shoals where weeds grow and clog up the channel later on with smelly, decaying vegetation. And lastly, what may sound rather carping criticism, modifications to river geometry do give a most unnatural look. Excessive use of sheet metal or concrete piling may give fine straight banks and speed up the velocity of the escaping floodwater but their aesthetic contribution to our towns is nil.

There are no statistics on flood fatalities. Flood deaths are not categorized as such in the International Classification of Diseases, Injuries and Causes of Death but are lumped under the heading of 'Cataclysm'. The numbers are fortunately extremely small, and of those that do occur, most have been through the disasters of breached dams or tidal flooding as at Lynmouth in 1953. It is the possibility of this type of catastrophe happening again that has prompted the building of the Thames Barrage. If a river out of control is frightful enough, it becomes much worse when the forces of the sea are added to it. There is a real chance of freak storms and a high tide occurring when the Thames is in full spate. If this happened, large areas of London would quickly be submerged.

As a result of records noted at London Bridge since 1791 we know that freak high tide levels, known as surge tides, are on the increase.

This seems to be due to a variety of factors. Firstly, mainland Britain is slowly tilting along an axis from Bristol to Newcastle, and secondly the volume of the world's oceans seems to be on the increase. Waves also move down the Thames more quickly because dredging has improved the shape of its channel.

During the notorious 1953 surge, when hundreds of people were killed in south-east England, the tide was six feet higher than predicted. It took nearly another twenty years to get the go-ahead for the construction of the Thames Barrage to prevent a similar disaster happening in London. This scheme has two components: raised flood embankments lining the banks downstream and a barrier across the Woolwich Reach. The massive concrete structure has ten gates pivoted between piers. The outer gates can be shut completely while the four gates over the central part of the river spanning the four 61 metre wide navigational channels remain recessed in the bed (see Figure 21) until needed. This allows them to be raised through 90° to cut off the tidal surge completely or to be partially open so that the riverwater can continue its downstream passage to the sea.

The cost of the damage is obviously related to both frequency and severity of floods. Most flood estimation techniques are based on studying the previous behaviour of a river at a particular site. Past records of flood levels are checked against the rainfall that occurred at the time. Correlations between rainfall incidence and river rise allow an empirical estimate of flood risk to be made. The method is weak in that it assumes that the physical nature of the area has

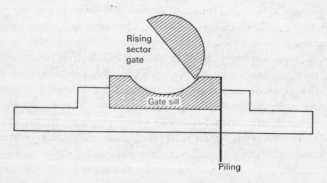

Figure 21   The Thames Barrage spanning Woolwich Reach.

remained the same since records began, that no new towns have been built or extensive agricultural development taken place to upset soil drainage patterns, and that reliable records exist of the site in question, which is not always the case.

There is also the problem of estimating flood risks at sites for which no records exist, a frequent situation in motorway design when bridges span streams in rural areas. A rough estimate of the area's flood susceptibility can be got from assessing those physical conditions of the area that are relevant to determining how much water has to drain away. The first and most obvious control is the size of the drainage basin itself: the bigger it is the more runoff it will generate. Next comes the layout of the drainage network, then the characteristics of the streams themselves, and finally the type of soil and how wet it is. These physical attributes are fed into appropriate mathematical equations, together with hypothetical rainfall inputs, to give estimates of the likely runoff. The larger the rainfall input the bigger the runoff, and so the point at which a flood situation is likely can be predicted.

There are rainfall statistics for the whole country going back to the last century, from which frequency and intensity possibilities, up to the physical maximum possible, can be used to calculate the frequency likelihood of floods of differing severity, the once-in-ten-years event, once-in-fifty, once-in-a-hundred and so on. The rainfall figures have to be weighted according to historic trends, the changing pattern of rainfall observed over the century. There are also certain patterns in rainfall incidence which lead to regional bias in the prediction equations. And since it is the cumulative effect of prolonged rain as well as intensity which is important, this has to be taken into account in the calculations. For example, rainstorms over the eastern side of the country more often than not die out after twelve hours. This is not so in the west, where the Londoner's hopeful adage, 'rain before seven, fine by eleven' probably falls on deaf ears if he is holidaying in the West Country or the Lake District. Indeed, our strange and erratic climate means that a whole gamut of climatic variables must be considered in some circumstances: it is not a physical impossibility in the UK for a severe thunderstorm to take place over a frozen catchment with deep snow cover – the Thames floods of 1947 were made much worse because the ground was frozen.

The influence of the catchment's physical nature on the type of flood generated is still imperfectly understood, however, and these sorts of calculation provide no more than a first rough estimate. This is illustrated by the flood on the River Lud in Lincolnshire where on 29 May 1920 just under five inches of rain fell in five hours, producing a fifteen foot rise in the river. The resulting flood was responsible for twenty-four deaths. According to theoretical estimation techniques, this size of storm could not possibly have produced a flood wave of such magnitude (the flood wave was some thirty-three times the maximum mean annual flow at that point on the Lud) or one that peaked so soon – an eye-witness account says the river rose six feet in ten minutes. Obviously hidden factors were operating which have never been identified.

Some flood risk problems need a more complete picture of the flood pattern, not just how high the levels will come and how often, but how long the water will take to reach its peak and how long the excess water will remain. This is particularly important with bridges and dams, for example. Here the calculations should indicate to the designer how often and how seriously his structure will be under stress and the point at which it is likely to fail.

Building costs being what they are, many minor structures have to have a specific risk factor assigned to them. Flood relief culverts and spillways or footbridges over streams have to be designed to cope with everything up to and including the most serious storm likely, say once in fifty or a hundred years, but not to withstand the most serious onslaught that the elements could ever produce. Such a conservative 'design life' would be totally inadequate for reservoir dams or motorway bridges which whatever happens must not succumb. No amount of erudite mathematical modelling can predict what has never actually happened before, and we cannot guess very accurately about future weather patterns. Thus gross underestimates can happen, unfortunately, and every decade has seen a dam disaster somewhere in the world.

Any ponding up of water above the natural ground level inevitably creates a risk situation. Dams on reservoirs built in this country have to be inspected regularly by an approved engineer in case the dam has been disturbed in any way or catchment conditions have changed since it was built. The regulations about inspection currently relate to

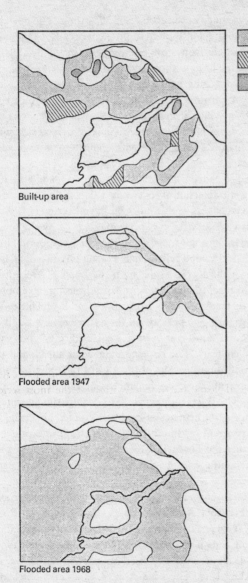

pre-1945

1945–65

post 1966

Built-up area

Flooded area 1947

Flooded area 1968

Figure 22   A case history of floods at East Molesey.

an Act passed in 1930, but a new version is in the offing. The new Act is expected to cost about £1 million to implement because of the extra inspection work required; from now on no reservoir will be allowed to fill beyond the design limit without special dispensation certificates. Here we seem to be dragging behind the United States, who started a crash inspection programme as a result of the Toccoa dam disaster at the end of 1977, in which thirty-nine people were killed. Several reservoirs had their water levels lowered because of defects that were discovered in 'high hazard' dams, those with communities just down-stream.

The River Mole in Surrey flows into the River Thames at East Molesey, almost opposite Hampton Court Palace. The combined floodplains of the two rivers at this junction have been very heavily built over in the last century or so. The damage done by the severe flood of March 1947, although mostly confined to areas round Hurst Park Racecourse, led to a flood relief scheme being put into operation on the lower part of the River Mole, with the hope of preventing similar damage in future. In 1960 pressure from housing developers, with the promise of fringe benefits from shops and a much needed school, forced the granting of permission for extensive new building work, despite a local inquiry at which local authority and river engineers voiced their fears. The development went ahead, and the precaution was taken of raising part of the area of the old racecourse by infilling. In September 1968 seven inches of rain fell in under twenty-four hours. The rivers did their best to contain this enormous volume of water but 1,014 hectares of land went under, affecting ten thousand homes. A rough estimate of the damage done came to £1,300,000. Since then the Thames Conservancy has built a new flood relief scheme to accommodate levels equal to the 1968 flow, and costing £2,067,000.

Before you wag admonishing fingers at greedy developers, how-ever, reflect that this story nicely illustrates the fallibility of flood estimation. The post-1947 relief scheme was based on the situation operating at that time and on the worst flood then experienced; having taken these precautions it was very hard to resist plans to release much-needed building land. The 1968 disaster, as it turns out, has a likely return period of two hundred years. But that is just statistical jargon, and all that can be claimed is a greater measure of security than existed before. The cost of such insurance is the price we have to pay for thumbing our noses at the elements.

What can we do about droughts? Not much in the short term, as we find out every summer when the hosepipe bans come into force. All reservoir schemes are planned with drought conditions in mind. The critical design factor is the ability of the reservoir to meet demand for an eighteen-month period during which streamflow is below average. By 'average' in this context we mean the driest years on record. These used to be 1933–5; now of course they are 1975 and 1976. You may well ask why it is that hosepipe bans are so frequent if the design strategy is based on such rare events. The answer is that water authorities hope that by imposing slight restrictions at the first hint of trouble, they will avoid the need to impose more stringent conditions later. After all, they know no more than we do when the next rain will fall and whether this is the year they will witness the longest drought on record. Once the water has gone, it has gone for good, hence the ever-ready hand poised over the stopcocks.

Drought studies, like flood studies, look at long-term records and relate the severity of past droughts to the conditions prevailing at the time. Obviously rainfall input – or rather the lack of it – is the overriding influence. After that, the underlying geology of the area is important, for this determines the base flow from groundwater sources and may make a difference to the rate at which the flow dwindles when the drought really begins to bite.

Now that there are so many integrated river systems where the riverflow has to be controlled according to reservoir capacities or sewage effluent input, the low flow performance of the river under drought conditions has to be forecast as precisely as when it is running at full spate or flooding. A particularly important feature is the river's ability to dilute the effluents discharged into it. Here the initial factor is not only the lowest flow likely but the persistence of minimal levels, for a dilution rate that improves after eight days will have a very different effect on the way a river recovers from concentrated pollution than one which takes eighty days. Likewise, there are different medical implications arising from short doses of carcinogenic toxins than from situations where there are constant background levels.

So far neither individuals nor organizations have often felt it necessary to insure against too little water. However, the 1975–6 drought brought with it not only embarrassingly empty reservoirs but also a four-fold increase in insurance claims for subsidence damage. This was caused by differential settlement on over-consolidated clays, particularly in the south-east. Thirsty trees were blamed for much of the damage to houses, since a full-grown tree can extract up to 15,000 litres of water from the soil in a reasonably hot summer. The most notorious species are poplars and willows with their extensive root systems, which often reach out more than twice the height of the tree. The drying rate of clay soils during drought periods also has disastrous effects on metalled roads, and most south-eastern county councils have had a bigger road repair bill than usual in the late 1970s.

6 *Water Management Today*

Water supply started off as a local affair with independent water undertakings set up either as private companies or as municipally controlled water boards and corporations. Twenty-eight private concerns are still in operation, although a Government White Paper has been published calling for their nationalization, which will bring them within the current regional water authority network.

At the other end of the scale the wastewater disposal service likewise grew up in a parochial fashion, the sewage authorities this time coming under the local government machine. The third aspect of water management, the control of the rivers, has the longest history of all. First attempts at river management go back to 1427, when the first Sewer Commissions were formed. These were originally set up to promote land drainage and the prevention of floods, usually in tidal areas. Along specific reaches they inevitably became involved in disputes between upstream and downstream users, such as those between bargees and mill-owners.

The administrative machinery gradually evolved from river boards, mainly concerned with navigation and development of water resources for their river catchment area. Increasing demand for water and attempts at formulating land use policies revealed embarrassing gaps in vital information about the varying water yield of natural catchments. This led to the Water Act of 1963, which enforced the setting up of hydrometric schemes, making it obligatory for the river authorities to collect a whole range of measurements related to their rivers.

Simultaneous with the creation of the new river authorities was the birth of an organization called the Water Resources Board. This board, although a government agency responsible for advising the Minister for Housing and Local Government on national water policy, soon established for itself a reputation for hard thinking and plain words, turning out the sort of reports not usually associated with conservative engineering organizations. The board's main task was to work out a national policy for water resources based on the information now coming in from the twenty-nine river authorities through their hydrometric networks, the population projections, extrapolation of industrial demand, changing patterns in agricultural production, and so on. The board tried to assist the river authorities with suggestions for the conservation, redistribution and augmentation of the water resources of their river areas. Time and time again, however, the proposals came to nothing because the authorities were financially powerless to implement new schemes or to cope with the complex problem of increasing effluent discharge.

The Water Resources Board, acting as though it were a body with independent democratic status, only made matters worse by revealing the true complexity of the choices facing the industry. The strong public concern over the use of land for water, for example inundating unspoilt countryside in non-industrial areas, led to many new schemes foundering because of the effectiveness of the local preservation societies. These lobbied MPs and caused proposals to be rejected by Parliament even though they had been approved by the appropriate government department. As the river authorities had no statutory obligation to meet rising consumer demand, the result was stalemate.

The board's forward thinking during the 1960s had to reflect the growing concern over the need to conserve land and gave special emphasis to regulating reservoirs and pumped storage schemes. These were not only a sop to public opinion but also had more flexibility – at a price. As they depend on abstracting water from the lower reaches of the rivers, they encounter greater effluent problems, not just in terms of bulk but also because adequate treatment of the newer sorts of industrial waste is not easy. The hair-raising consequences of accidental spillage of some noxious industrial chemicals have on many occasions been avoided only through quick action by waterworks staff.

Bringing together the Ministries of Housing and Local Government, Transport, and Public Building and Works into the vast organization of the Department of the Environment took place in 1970 with the change to a Tory Government. Even right-wing politicians could not resist the chance to keep an eye on the water industry and so there was set up a Directorate General Water Engineering within the Department to advise both Government and industry on water supply, wastewater treatment and dispersal. This was the death knell for the Water Resources Board, subsequently disbanded in 1973 with the passing of a new Water Act.

Things happen only slowly in resource planning and it takes up to twenty-five years from the drawing board stage to the turning of the tap for new water supplies. Throughout its ten-year life the Water Resources Board had been almost hysterical in its constant pressure to get Government agreement on the long-term strategy necessary to meet the expected demands of the next century. Before its demise it had the satisfaction of realizing that at least there was to be an administrative reorganization which could implement many of its ideas. Its various reports had shown that much of the extra water needed could come by manipulating what we already have. But to do this, fresh and foul water control must work harmoniously. On the grounds that any organization would think twice about pumping substandard effluent into the nearest watercourse when it had also to use that water for its customers, the Act did away with all the existing bodies (except the private water companies) and replaced the lot with regional water authorities. The 29 river authorities, 157 water undertakings and 1,393 sewerage and sewage disposal units operating in England and Wales were absorbed into just ten large regional organizations, responsible for all aspects of water, from source to sewer. In Scotland 12 authorities have replaced over 200 local water authorities and 234 local sewerage authorities.

Under the terms of the Water Act 1973, the nine regional water authorities and the Welsh Water authority are responsible for the provision of all water services in their regions – water resource development, water supply (in association with twenty-eight private water companies supplying some 25 per cent of the population), sewerage and sewage disposal, river conservation, pollution control, land drainage, fisheries, and some navigation and water-based recreation. Their sewerage responsibilities are generally discharged through the agency of district and certain other councils. In Scotland all water and sewerage services except pollution control and fisheries are the responsibility of local government, i.e. nine regional and three islands

Figure 23   Areas of regional water authorities – set up after the 1973 Water Act. Note that, following the fashion set by other utilities, the word 'Authority' is often dropped in promotional literature, with the authorities calling themselves simply 'Thames Water', Welsh Water', etc.

councils, aided by the Central Scotland Water Development Board. The remaining functions are exercised by ten River Purification Boards.

Each of the ten authorities is based on entire river catchment areas, not sticking to the administrative boundaries followed by local or national government agencies. The political view at the time of the changeover was that 'Ministers believe in the importance of strong regional bodies. Water services is not a sphere where we need excessive centralization. This does not mean that there are no national issues but that many problems will be best solved at regional level.'

Ministerial responsibility for water in fact rests with two government departments, the Department of the Environment for supply and disposal, and the Ministry of Agriculture for land drainage and flood control, an ancient commitment which they are loath to relinquish despite attempts to get all water responsibility within a single ministry. The existing split between 'high flows' and 'low flows' certainly does not help integrated planning and calls for much cross-representation on committees. Initially, the members of each regional authority were appointed either by the Secretary of State for the Environment or by the Minister of State for Agriculture, or nominated by the local authorities within the regions concerned. This resulted in boards with up to sixty members. These people were not elected and thus not accountable to the people whom they served, although meetings were held in public.

The latest reorganization in water management is towards a drastic reduction in membership, with Government proposals for only nine to fifteen members for each authority, all to be selected by central government and meeting in private. The reason given is to save money and reduce bureaucracy. Apparently, contributions made by local government nominees were disappointing and so public interests would be better served by consumer bodies: at the time of writing (1983), precise details of how these might function have yet to be announced.

There was also a central organization, the National Water Council. The N W C's job was to advise Ministers on matters of national policy and to promote and assist the efficient performance by water authorities of their functions through centrally-organized training programmes, information services, etc. The Council's main activity in Scotland was restricted to training and testing of water equipment. The National Water Council has now been abolished, probably on political grounds because of its 'failures' (in a Tory government's eyes) to curtail recent industrial action by water workers. The water industry has therefore been slapped down quite harshly by central government. The public relations in the early years of the new large authorities were not too good because of the awkward shortages in some regions during the 1975–6 drought. To be fair, they were unlucky in having to cope with an unprecedented supply situation so soon after putting up all the water charges. Whether or not there is a need for a central body is a moot point. Each regional authority is expected to solve the problems and conflicting interests of its own area as best it may; it is not directed in detail how to go about its business. Except, and this is a key issue, each one is expected to be self-financing by charging for water supply, sewerage and other services. There is a long-standing statutory obligation, inherited from the old boards and corporations, to provide wholesome water in adequate quantities to domestic consumers, and to provide water on reasonable terms for non-domestic consumers, provided this does not involve unreasonable expenditure on constructing new waterworks.

However, responsibility for the nation's water is not left to the R W As alone. In that it is the duty of every local authority to ascertain the sufficiency and wholesomeness of supplies in its area, this provision is acknowledged to be a public health service and it is the local government machine which has to take full responsibility for safe water. This split in responsibilities inevitably provokes conflict.

The water industry has always claimed to be the most capital-intensive industry in the land. The annual investment required for the renewal and maintenance of existing services will not alter that claim. Recent cutbacks in government spending, however, although not affecting the water industry directly, have meant that restraint has had to be exercised and specific capital expenditure allocations set by the Government have determined spending ceilings. This means that, for example, the expenditure by the Water Authorities in 1983-4 will be only 52 per cent of that in 1973-4 in real terms, which is bound to have most effect on investment and capital projects.

Scope for economies in the industry is of course pretty limited. Most of the costs are fixed, tied to the running of treatment plants and sewage works and keeping the supply system intact. Some fairly massive manpower cuts have been enforced in recent years, as they have in many of the other utilities. One of the biggest headaches is the budgeting for the fluctuating interest rates on borrowed money. The income from present water charges to domestic and industrial users does not in any way cover the cost of water supply and disposal. Each year large sums are ear-marked as interest on old debts, since only about 3 per cent of outstanding debt is redeemed each year. Virtually all capital expenditure, whether for renewals or improvements, comes from new borrowing arrangements: about 40 per cent of total costs are interest charges, equivalent to twice the industry's manpower costs.

The more outspoken of the R W A executives say they want to halt this 'use now, pay later' policy by increasing water charges to bring them in line with real costs. The kind of figure currently being bandied about is a 20 per cent increase (which does not include any adjustments for inflation). The alternative, they say, is to cut construction investment by 40 per cent, the most likely outcome of which will be a rapid deterioration in the sewerage system. Some relief would be achieved by charging the costs of new works – water mains and drainage – to the new houses and factories which create the demand. The effect would be to reduce the borrowing load by about 35 per cent and, at today's prices, add an average of about £1,000 to the cost of a new house. Charitably, the proponents of such schemes say that once users are paying real costs they could then choose which improvements they consider essential to the services they get, the implication being that the public could influence future growth patterns. One cannot help feeling that this might end up like the railways, where money talks loudest: long-distance freight and inter-city high-income lines keep going while rural communities suffer. With water, health reasons would prevent extreme curtailment of services, but costs might seriously alter future devolution patterns.

Part of the problem, the industry argues, is that being public bodies they are forced to raise money through the National Loans Fund. The private water companies (responsible for about 22 per cent of total water supplied) who have clung to their independence and will continue to fight against nationalization, can as private organizations borrow their money at much cheaper rates.

The dramatic increases in water rates during the last decade following the 1973 Water Act and the setting up of the Regional Water Authorities were partly due to the loss in revenue from the Rate Support Grant which subsidized local authority spending in sewerage and sewage disposal, partly due to inflation – the money committed for capital schemes cost a lot more – and partly that charges had been held down previously as a contribution to national counter-inflation policies, something no longer relevant now the R W As are required to be self-financing. The outcry over increased rates for country properties not connected to mains drainage led to rate relief in such cases, adding an extra 26 per cent to sewerage charges to be shared out among the rest. However, water services are now substantially independent of subsidies from either general rates or national taxes.

A long-term effect of the public concern was to provoke Parliament in December 1976 to bring in a Water Charges Equalization Bill to reduce the disparity between the rates charged by the ten different authorities, at one stage as much as 61 per cent between regions. The Bill also balanced the legacy of debts raised by the authorities. The central National Water Council acted as banker, taking from areas with large incomes such as the Thames Water Authority and giving to those having to charge higher rates such as the Welsh authority. Although while in operation the Bill brought in £3 million to the Welsh, it was abolished in 1980 as it was really no more than a political move designed to calm public feelings about 'Welsh' water going to England where it then 'cost' less than it did at its point of origin, since the equalization charges were restricted to unmeasured water supplies. Consequently, the bill did not help the industry in any practical way, such as by promoting a truly national water supply. The more general service charges, industrial sewage, sewage disposal and a string of amenity services were not equalized, on the grounds that different authorities have different effluent standards to meet and, by contrast with water supply, each area is self-sufficient in sewage disposal. Metered supplies to industry were also omitted on the grounds that industry can look after itself: it is free to go wherever the water is cheapest or to economize by introducing ways to cut down on use. The water authorities themselves say that equalization charges should include all water and sewage charges, not just unmetered supplies. Meanwhile the Northumbrian, Thames and North West Water Authorities took matters into their own hands and introduced a system of direct billing just like the other public utilities, so that from April 1978 consumers have had to pay for all water services provided – supply, disposal, pollution control, etc. This brings about 'savings' by speeding up the cash flow and thus reducing payments on money that would otherwise have to be borrowed.

The enforced liaison between the water authorities and local government councils over waste disposal was one of the least successful outcomes of the 1973 Act. The main area of friction was over sewerage problems. This is probably due to the general financial situation as much as anything but the fact remains that the R W As resented having to contract work to local government agents over whom they had little financial or technical control.

The local authorities felt the opposite, that sewerage could not be divorced from planning and design of housing or industrial sites and that sewage treatment should be funded through the General Rate. In the event, the R W As won the day and they now have agency arrangements with the local government bodies and the power to do the work themselves if they so wish. It is now the water authorities, not the local authority, who empty cesspools charging 50 per cent of the economic cost of the service to the householder, over and above the water rate.

Unlike many other industries, the water industry actually has a policy of discouraging use of its product. This is quite different from the situation in the USA, for example, where both public and privately-owned water undertakings operate. There, as might be expected, the investment-backed companies meter their customers and positively encourage greater use, even during periods of drought.

There is no sign of any change in the rating system for domestic properties, so, as from 1 April 1982, all households have the option to have their water metered and pay on a volume basis if they feel their rates are unfair. Indeed, water authorities are empowered to meter domestic users and supply on a volume basis if they so wish.

The only place in the UK which has had universal water metering is the town of Malvern in Worcestershire. The scheme was abandoned in 1969, only to be restarted by the Department of the Environment more recently as an experiment, to get more detailed information on the pattern and quantity of domestic demand. We can compare the path followed by the electricity industry. Here the boards originally started with a flat-rate charge based on the number of points or rooms in a house. As prices increased it was obviously neither sensible nor equitable to continue charging on a flat-rate basis.

There appears to be little scope for cutting down domestic use, even if such savings are considered desirable. The impassioned pleas to save water during the 1975–6 drought only brought about savings of the order of 15–20 per cent so it seems that there is comparatively little wasted or squandered during normal supply periods. If that is so, then consumption would be little affected by metering, the cost of which is enormous, about £50 per house per year plus another £10 for the cost of inspection. Nationally, this amounts to some £500 million, about the same amount as that estimated for bringing sewage and industrial effluents up to the standards set for the 1980s. However it has been argued that in the Netherlands, a country with similar levels of demand, metering has produced a consumption rate a third less than ours.

There is nevertheless a keen interest in metering among water engineers, for this is probably the only way of detecting the extent of losses in distribution systems. Figures varying from 20 to 50 per cent from some of the older conurbations have been quoted for years, but accurate quantities are not really known. Certainly, the Malvern experiment shows that 31 per cent of the water entering one end of the distribution system is not accounted for by the consumer meters.

While loss assessment based on meter figures is not particularly accurate, it is interesting to compare the 5–53 per cent 'loss' figures available from different parts of this country with the 5 per cent quoted for rebuilt Hamburg, the 17 per cent for Brussels and over 50 per cent for Bangkok. A better method is to gauge night flow to one area in the small hours of the night. Some of the amount will be used to fill storage reservoirs or cisterns of automatic flushing toilets and other legitimate industrial uses. However, the volume passing through is seldom less than 10 per cent of the average daily flow and is often up to 25 per cent, a figure far in excess of likely uses, and a fair indication that distribution systems are very leaky indeed.

The losses due to leakage are a nagging problem for the maintenance crews with so much of the urban installations dating from the turn of the century or earlier. Not only are many of these pipes fracturing with old age or vibration from heavier and heavier traffic through our towns, but also much of the original network has been lost.

Here I can quote an example from personal experience. A foot of water appeared suddenly in the cellars beneath our house one January a few years ago, and persisted for several weeks. Both the local council and the water authority understandably tried to convince us that it was just floodwater from the heavy rain that winter. Luckily for us, the foreman of the water authority's repair gang said that he knew cellars in Wallingford had no history of flooding and that he was certain there was a leak somewhere. Over the next few weeks he methodically checked the mains pipes in the street, using his 'listening stick' to detect the sound of running water. Sure enough, about a hundred yards away, in the courtyard of the doctor's surgery, he found it. Two feet below ground was an old water main with a branch heading off towards the town park, from which water was pouring out. What building it was supposed to serve no one knows. The pipe was sealed up, the water disappeared from the cellar, and no complaints have been received from deprived householders.

According to this foreman, the engineers from all the services – gas, electricity, telephone and water – are often faced with a bewildering array of unmarked cables and pipes when they dig their holes. Even if they manage to complete their specific task without damaging the other pipes they expose, the trouble comes with the backfilling operations, when the soil is rammed home in the trenches.

Since 1936 local drainage authorities have been supposed by law to keep maps showing public sewers, a duty often neglected. One local Public Health Inspector tells of futile attempts to trace the path of some disused sewers by using tracer dyes. So far, not a speck of several bucketfuls of chemical poured down has ever shown up again.

It is only recently that householders have become liable to prosecution if they neglect leaking or defective fittings on their own premises. There is certainly room for improvement in conventional plumbing fittings; there could so easily be a better type of valve than a ballcock, for instance. It is a salutary thought that a dripping tap may lose as much as 10 gallons (45 litres) of water a night.

Alongside this type of common sense improvement even the WC is being scrutinized. The amount of potable water used for flushing WCs is estimated at 650 million gallons (3,000 cubic metres) per day in England and Wales out of a total public supply of 3,300 million gallons (10,652 thousand cubic metres) per day, making the WC the largest single consumer of water. The simple and effective way of cutting down on the amount of water needed for flushing is to put a polythene bag filled with water in the cistern – as indeed many people were persuaded to do during the drought's water-saving campaign. This was a simple demonstration that the two-gallon flush is somewhat over-generous. Even this is better than in Scotland, where three-gallon cisterns are the norm.

Experimental dry toilets which work by vacuum, composting or incinerating the waste all have the disadvantage of needing an energy supply, usually electricity. Not much saving there unless it is of the order of the overall energy requirement for pumping water at some point in the distribution network. Water-saving cisterns have just been installed in some houses in Wiltshire as an experiment. Wessex Water Authority want to find out whether it would be cheaper to convert cisterns throughout its area or to face the enormous costs of yet more water supply in the future. The new style cisterns are either dual flush, which give a full two-gallon flush or a one-gallon flush as needed, or a version which only flushes as long as the handle is pressed and can therefore be stopped as soon as the pan is clear. Once the problem of the cistern is solved, washing machines and dishwashers can be looked at to see what savings might be possible there.

For many years now those directly concerned with water supplies have grumbled that water is too cheap, that the public expects too much for the small amount of money it gives them. Part of the trouble may well be an inherent fault in the planning aspects of the industry itself. For all new projects are evaluated on a cost-minimization basis, rather than benefit-maximization, because of the sheer complexity of trying to put a market price on spinoff benefits such as the extra recreational opportunities provided by a new reservoir scheme. However, it is possible to use a loss function to calculate the economic or monetary loss which results if certain criteria about quantity or quality of the water to be provided by the new scheme are not met. Restricting water supply in urban centres might for instance cut future industrial expansion and so cause loss, or water which failed to meet predetermined quality standards might need treating at extra cost. This is something which will need close watching in future as water is transferred on a bigger scale through regulating reservoirs or inter-regional transfers.

A big difficulty facing any planner is coming to terms with the fact that the capacity of any water source cannot be assumed to be a finite figure. Instead, he must accept that design capacity also relates to security of supply. In other words, for 90 per cent of the time much more is available than for say 99 per cent. Modern resource management therefore relies on the conjunctive use of sources of different types (surface or groundwater), even from different geographical regions if distribution networks are feasible, to provide a total capacity greater than the sum of individual sources with a given degree of security. This introduces a whole range of difficult design and operational decisions. Some would go so far as to advocate charging a higher price for 'secure' water than for the rest.

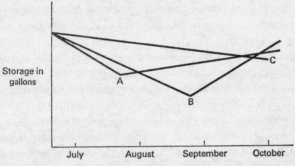

Figure 24 The problems of day-to-day management are shown in this simplified situation. Compared with average yearly depletion of resources (C), an assessment of the current situation in July would make year (A) seem much worse than year (B), although retrospectively the latter would be much more serious.

A more mundane feature of water management that keeps hitting the technical press headlines is the nagging problem of the nation's sewers. So much of the vast underground network, that we forget about since it is buried out of sight, was installed when our towns and cities expanded in the last half of the last century. It has been neglected ever since. We assume that once installed and subsequently built over sewers are indestructible. Nothing is further from the truth. Inevitably, as construction costs have escalated, repair and replacement needs have been allowed to slip, to the extent that vast tracts of the country's sewers need renovating or replacing *now*. The longer the task is put off, the greater the frequency with which damaged sewers collapse, often taking with them other essential service pipes and cables.

If we assume that the pipes and conduits have an average life of ninety to a hundred years, with a constant rate of installation the country's commitment to replacements alone should be at least 1 per cent of the annual expenditure for water resources. In fact, the situation is a little worse than this because about 15 per cent of sewers are known to be over a hundred years old. On current figures this calls for an annual rate of spending of at least £310 million a year to maintain the system in its existing state, for, in replacement terms, the asset value of our sewers is £31 billion (1983 figures). This takes into account the 234,000 kilometres of regional water authority sewers and the estimated further 200,000 kilometres of buried pipes of the highway authorities.

New methods of construction and repair are desperately needed. By and large, the bigger the sewer, the longer its life. The problem comes with the small-diameter range of pipes, some 93 per cent of the total, which has until now been inaccessible to inspection procedures and renovation. The reasons why sewers fail are either hydraulic overloading, exacerbated by growth in housing and industrial development and extension of 'impervious' surfaces in built-up areas, or the physical deterioration which comes with age, ground subsidence, heavy traffic, damage in excavation, and so on. Failures have to be put right at great cost; not only that of the repairs themselves, but in terms of the disturbance and strain put on other services. A further major difficulty is simply knowing where these sewers are, let alone their condition. The Anglian Water Authority, for instance, consider that they have an adequate knowledge of only about 8 per cent of the 22,000 kilometres of sewers in their area, in spite of the fact that well over half of them were built since 1945. This aspect makes the obvious answer of renovation before repair becomes necessary (usually half the cash cost) not so easy to implement. Several forms of relining are available, though the techniques are in their infancy and it is on this subject that most engineering research will be concentrated for many years to come.

The next problem for attention concerns the quality of water in the sewer network, since ultimately much of it is destined to return to our taps. The first sewer networks were designed to collect both foul water from drains and the rainwater entering down gutters from roads and pavements. Such combined systems are prevalent in older conurbations, where the whole of the sewer water passes through treatment works before being returned to the nearest watercourse. From the mid-1920s onwards, however, the tendency has been to separate the two types of effluent, making foul water from mains drainage go to the sewage works and surface water from stormwater drainage go directly to the river. The extra costs of dual pipe installations are balanced against volumes of effluent needing treatment. Recently, however, people have begun to worry about the quality of the storm sewer water, which in theory ought to be pretty clean. Analysis of this type of water at the river outfall shows that in many cases its purity is far below that of treated sewage effluent. The causes are hard to pinpoint exactly, but for example the pouring of waste sump oil down the nearest road grating by those who do their own car maintenance is the kind of activity which certainly does not help.

Domestic wastes are relatively simple to cope with, being mostly nitrogen- and phosphorus-based derivatives. The usual figures quoted are a daily excretion of 9 grams of nitrogen and 2 grams of phosphorus per person, the nitrogen mostly in an organic form which is readily removed during the primary sedimentation process at the sewage works. On a volume basis, the total sewage load for England and Wales is 14 million cubic metres of liquid a day, about a third of which comes from domestic sources, being equivalent to 136 litres per head of population. Sewage sludge, the output 'product' of all Britain's sewage works, amounts to 1.25 metric tons dry weight annually, and disposal of this accounts for over 50 per cent of the total waste water treatment costs. This could be even more expensive in future, as the European Community proposes tighter controls on land application of sewage sludge as a safeguard against the health hazards from metal contamination.

The effluent from the sewage works ultimately goes into the nearest appropriate watercourse. Rivers are able to cleanse themselves and purify their water because of the dissolved oxygen present. Not only does flowing water pick up oxygen from the atmosphere but it also gains some through the photosynthetic activity of plants and algae. Bacteria present in the water and in the sediment of the riverbed are able to feed on most of the pollution substances, which they do effectively so long as there is abundant oxygen available. Shallow, turbulent streams pick up more oxygen than deeper, slower-moving rivers; lakes and ponds are efficient because of the large surface area for this oxygen pick-up. But if the concentration of extraneous substances in the water of the river gets too high, all the oxygen is used up in the oxygenation process and the river can no longer cope. The lack of oxygen not only stops the cleansing process but also kills off the plant life, overloading the bacterial population trying to decompose the plant residues as well as the polluting substances, and the whole system spirals down into stagnation. Rivers, like people, therefore get sick through taking in toxic substances. The cure is the same too, rest and the right treatment; the longer the 'illness', the more difficult the treatment becomes.

For years now Government and the water industry alike have paid lip-service to the notion of cleaning up rivers by establishing strict controls on the quality of water allowed to enter natural open watercourses. The most notorious examples of badly polluted rivers are the River Calder and the River Trent, the latter potentially an invaluable source of water for the Midlands if only it could be cleaned up. Over half the nation's sewage works are turning out unsatisfactory effluent. The River Tyne, for example, receives 320 million litres of untreated sewage every day, which is about the volume of freshwater flow down the river during minimum flow periods. This is because only 5 per cent of the sewage from the one million inhabitants of Tyneside is treated before it goes into the river. To control this and similar situations the Government brought in a Control of Pollution Act in 1974: in 1983 the sections relating to water pollution were still not implemented and only those aspects bearing directly on the UK's obligations to conform with EEC directives are expected to be phased in by 1986. The National Water Council downgraded the quality standard the Act sets for effluent discharges in an attempt to protect the individual authorities from continual prosecution under the Act, since economic pressure means they simply cannot improve some of the worst offending rivers overnight. The Department of the Environment figures on polluted water courses reveal that 2,914 kilometres were bad in 1975, equivalent to 8 per cent of the total surveyed. By 1980 the percentage figure had only improved to 7 per cent, for, although the extent of 'grossly polluted' water was much less, there were correspondingly much larger stretches coming under the 'doubtful' and 'poor' categories. Things are however improving. In

Table 4   Classification of Rivers – as defined by the Department of the Environment (DOE)

Class 1	Unpolluted or recovered from pollution. Biological oxygen demand (BOD) generally less than 3 milligrams per litre and well oxygenated.
Class 2	Doubtful quality. Reduced oxygen content, containing turbid or toxic discharges but not seriously affected.
Class 3	Poor quality. Dissolved oxygen below 50 per cent saturation for considerable periods, occasionally toxic and changed in character by the discharge of solids.
Class 4	Grossly polluted. BOD greater than 12, incapable of supporting fish life, smelling and offensive in appearance.

1957 the Natural History Museum carried out a survey of the Thames from Richmond to Gravesend and could find no evidence of any fish present at all; over ninety species have been caught since, starting in 1963 and including one salmon (which sits in stuffed splendour in a glass case at the Thames Water Authority's headquarters). We are still a long way off from the conditions in the eighteenth century, however, when salmon were so plentiful in the Thames that apprentices of London protested that they ate nothing else. The worst offenders have been war-damaged sewers and hard detergents which inhibited natural oxygenation. The latter have now been phased out. There is still concern over thermal pollution from the twenty Thames-side power stations and the planned doubled capacity for these by the year 2000 will slow progress down.

The National Water Council wanted the RWAs to be able to establish river quality objectives for all their rivers and to fix individual discharge content on the basis of these objectives instead of on the fixed standards set by the Royal Commission on Environmental Pollution. This body has come up with a blanket optimum value of 30 milligrams per litre of suspended solids, 20 milligrams per litre of

Table 5   Biological Oxygen Demand and Stream Condition

Stream condition	5-day BOD (mg/l)
Very clean	1
Clean	2
Fairly clean	3
Doubtful	5
Bad	10

The Royal Commission on Environmental Pollution says that rivers need a BOD of less than 4 milligrams per litre to be free from pollution. This means that to keep streams clean, sewage effluent with a BOD of 20 milligrams per litre (and suspended solids content below 30 milligrams per litre) needs diluting at least 8 − 1 with clean water (2 milligrams per litre). Where this dilution ratio is not possible, more stringent effluent standards are needed to keep rivers in a satisfactory condition.

BOD (Biological Oxygen Demand − the depletion of oxygen in solution brought about by the biochemical breakdown of organic matter by microorganisms over a period of five days at a constant temperature of 20°C: expressed as milligrams per litre). The authorities argue that it is pointless spending vast sums to attain a high degree of purity and then let the water run into a stream at a lower standard. Indeed, even the Royal Commission admitted in a 1973 report that trout from the Tees would be a luxury that the unemployed of a depressed Teesside could ill afford. It is unreasonable to expect that any fixed standard can be maintained indefinitely and 95 per cent limits are allowed in the legislation.

The problem will be, the authorities fear, that the more unscrupulous industrial concerns may meet the standards most of the time but save up their worst effluents for discharge in one vast flush, with disastrous effects. This leads to another controversial issue: should we force individual firms to install their own treatment plant to remove toxic chemicals at source, or build more extensive and efficient sewage and treatment works operated on a fee basis by the water authorities for the benefit of all industry in an area? For industries whose effluent includes chemicals difficult to treat the cost of effluent plant is often prohibitive. A Huddersfield chemical manufacturer producing dyestuffs has sought Government aid to pay for the $£\frac{1}{2}$ million worth of equipment needed to reduce his effluent to the standard demanded by the Yorkshire Water Authority.

In many instances firms get round their problems by using the services of the industrial waste disposal firms that have mushroomed in the last decade. In the early years of their activities there were plenty of disused quarries, sand and gravel pits to fill up, and the odd load of cyanide or electroplating effluent mixed up with building rubble and so on caused little concern. However, after several instances of groundwater and reservoir supplies becoming seriously contaminated and wells being put out of action, it now appears that 'safe' sites for the disposal of waste from the nation's factories are diminishing rapidly and not being replaced. At the present time there seems no alternative to the use of land disposal for much of the industrial waste and in fact controlled safe landfill is now endorsed as official government policy for dealing with waste disposal. Site licensing is one of the far-reaching control measures in the 1974 Control of Pollution Act. The key issue of course is to define 'safe' sites. The instances of pollution of underground water are sufficient to indicate that the water authorities are right to be conservative in their licensing powers.

Growing pressures on the waste disposal firms have encouraged them to seek alternative outlets, and the most recent idea is to press to be allowed use of underground aquifers to dilute and disperse their effluents. The reasoning behind this proposal is that as slow filtering through sands and gravels forms the basis of water treatment in sewage works, the same job could be done *in situ*, to allow a controlled level of local contamination. Understandably, water experts are not too happy about the idea and cite the following reasons for their concern. First, there is the problem of toxic substances being flushed from underground by exceptionally high rainfall. Next, there are fears about the long-term effects once the natural absorption capacity of the ground has been used up. And, since geological strata are often far from homogeneous, no survey can guarantee the flow rates for a particular site. Neither could a survey reveal the danger of short-circuiting the system through cracks and fissures in the underlying rock, which could allow highly concentrated slugs of pollutant to enter underground streams. The nightmare aspect of the problem is that once contaminated such water resources may have to be written off for ever.

Intensive farming units, where cattle, pigs or chickens are kept indoors, also produce considerable waste disposal problems. Such specialization often means that these factory farms do not have spare land capacity on which to spread the large amounts of dung produced. Sludge from sewage works, in theory a convenient and concentrated form of fertilizer, likewise is not always easy to dispose of. As farming land is worked more intensively, there are fewer and fewer occasions when it is convenient to allow muck-spreading on a wide scale. These practical problems are in addition to concern over pathogen transfer or the simple public nuisance aspect of smell. Sadly, there have had to be cutbacks in spending on treatment plant because the money is needed for mains and sewer replacements. Nor has the situation been helped by oil price rises upsetting the costing on sludge incinerators.

Perhaps more worrying for the future is the growing evidence of an upward trend in nitrate levels in both surface and groundwater. Levels were so high in the Thames and Lea, for instance, that there were fears about its potability during the low flow periods of the dry summer of 1976, and water extracted from these two sources had to be blended with water from elsewhere to bring the levels down within acceptable limits. Excessive quantities of nitrate in drinking water can cause methaemoglobinaemia in infants under the age of six months who are bottle-fed, the baby developing a blue colour. The condition is reversible if recognized soon enough but can lead to permanent damage to the tissues or to death. So it is obviously essential to keep nitrate levels down to those set by the World Health Organization. But where does the nitrate come from? By far the largest portion of nitrate arises from the biologically fixed atmospheric nitrogen. All organisms need nitrogen for protein metabolism as part of life and growth but only a few are able to use the inert atmospheric nitrogen directly. Certain soil bacteria are able to 'fix' nitrogen and so make it available to plants and thus to animal life through the food chains. The decaying plant matter keeps up the nitrate store in the soil for succeeding generations to use. Nitrate that is soluble, as it must be for plants to absorb it in solution through their roots, can also be moved through the leaching action of rain infiltrating the soil, and thus a certain proportion of nitrate is always to be found in natural

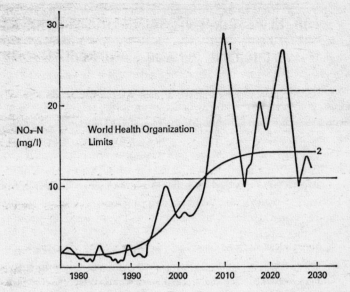

Figure 25 Models of nitrate concentration have been built up to predict future levels in groundwater. The validity of the models is checked by using them to predict tritium profiles. Tritium, an isotope of hydrogen, occurs naturally in the atmosphere but its concentration was considerably increased between 1950 and 1964 through releases from nuclear bomb tests. The tritium content of rainfall has a distinct pattern and can be recognized in soilwater profiles. Using such circumstantial evidence to determine the rate at which nitrate inputs from the surface might move down to the water table yields the sort of graphs shown above: (1) possible groundwater concentrations beneath fertilized arable/temporary grass ley and (2) average concentrations over a catchment area.

watercourses. Man upsets the delicate balance in pushing up the productivity of his crop plants by putting fertilizers on the land, whether inorganic or organic, such as farmyard manure or sewage sludge.

Existing radioactive tracing techniques used to plot water movement indicate that the nitrate trouble may stem from the increase in fertilizer use in the post-war years. As these same tracing techniques show that the downward rates of infiltration are often as little as one foot per year, it may be that the full impact of extra nitrate has not yet been felt, since the water table in the Chalk, for example, is often 80 feet down and in some rivers 90 per cent of base flow is of groundwater origin. Those who point the finger of blame at the farmers have to admit that the scant evidence is only circumstantial; the agricultural research workers springing to the defence of their industry say that any action which churns up the soil, whether it be through ploughshares or bulldozers, stimulates the release of nitrate through natural causes. There is limited evidence that in some water-bearing strata biological and chemical processes which can denitrify are operating, thereby making the whole matter much more complicated than many care to admit at the moment. The search for the suspected denitrifying bacteria carrying out such good works continues. Once identified, the next task will be to ascertain the rates at which they operate.

Likewise, another health hazard seems to be looming up as a result of unexpected side effects from tampering with the environment to suit our convenience. This time it is through the vastly increased use of salt on the roads during the winter months. Nowadays we resent any impediment to mobility and people are not prepared to wait for a thaw to make trunk roads less hazardous. Salt is very cheap and very effective for de-icing but there is little doubt that both sodium and chloride levels in water resources are on the increase. So far, experts in the UK are not too worried, but the states of Vermont and Massachusetts in the USA now have laws regulating the amount of salt that can be spread, because American scientists claim that high salt intake gives rise to cardio-vascular and hypertension disorders. In this country most highway authorities operate their salting practices on a rule-of-thumb basis and it is no exaggeration to say that most are over-salting two- or four-fold.

Until the water sources at fault were identified and taken out of commission, an unfortunate legacy of past industrial activity was the high incidence of insanity in localities with disused lead mines. Other upland sources have presented problems with goitre, caused by too much iodine in the water, and the effects of peat acids were disastrous when lead pipes were more common.

On the good side, depending on where you live, there is also the fact that hard water areas lose less of their male population from coronary thrombosis than do those with soft water. Such geographical benefits will have to be positively sought by those anxious about their health, however, because the hassle over fluoridation has probably deterred authorities from attempting similar prophylactic efforts for some time to come.

Keeping the nation's water fit to drink is the water engineer's prime job. As a double check, Medical Officers of Health with the local authorities have independent statutory responsibilities to see that the standards are maintained. But what standards? Amazingly there are no mandatory chemical or physical standards for UK water supplies. Many authorities conform to the World Health Organization's standards or those operated by the US Public Health Service, and EEC standards are being debated at the present time. Strict bacteriological controls are enforced but nevertheless some people consider this neglect of the chemical purity of drinking water extremely worrying. For example, there are an estimated eighty thousand homes in the country with a piped water supply having a lead content twice the World Health Organization level and four times that of the proposed EEC standards. The only way to remove such a potential health hazard is to rip out all the lead pipes. Economically, it would be cheaper to cut lead intake by reducing the lead content in petrol.

What we accept as potable water, whatever standards are used to measure it, is of course far from pure. Water is the most efficient solvent there is and pure H_2O simply does not exist in the natural state. The waterworks chemists check on the levels of specified compounds but as our society gets more advanced industrial processes there are likely to be many substances present in minute amounts which are not on their list but which ought to be monitored.

It is no good relying on single samples at infrequent intervals. There are, for instance, some elements whose concentration depends on whether they are precipitated out through the action of other chemicals in the water. This is the case with mercury, an element which mostly combines with other matter and falls out of solution but which can exist as methyl mercury and as such gets taken up in the food chains.

In the days when the main emphasis was on the exploitation of relatively pure upland reservoir water or clean groundwater, the existing screening process sufficed. The excellent medical health records of the British public proves it so. Now, however, planners say that future demand must lead to multiple reuse of water. This means more recycling, more pumped storage schemes downstream on our major rivers, even estuarial barrages, all implying that any pollutants entering the river system are likely to accumulate.

Dangerous organic residue can no doubt be identified and removed, but medical opinion is not yet united on which are potentially dangerous. It could be that if in the future consumers are told that their drinking water comes to them third- or even fourth-hand, they may well insist on better quality standards, even if the water must then cost more. Planners may think they are right to insist on reuse as the optimum course in the search for the cheapest water but possibly they might be surprised to find that the public, if they were asked, would prefer them to err on the side of safety.

7   Will We Manage Tomorrow?

As well as upheaving the various water supply responsibilities, the 1973 Water Act also asked for surveys of future demand and plans for meeting any shortfall to be prepared. These Section 24 surveys have occupied much of the time of the resource planning divisions of each authority ever since. Over and above these regional plans there have been several national reviews and commentaries on the correct water strategy. Increasingly, as population projections have shrunk and the money supply has got tighter, the emphasis has shifted from finding new sources and ambitious interregional transfers to concern about failing services and the need for adequate renovation and replacement of ageing structures.

The demand-forecasting necessary includes analysis of the components of domestic use, how to cope with increasing effluent, and the likely impact of increased charges on industrial demand. Although current estimates are for a rate of increase of about 1 per cent per annum, much, much less than the projections made in the 1960s when some of the large reservoirs to come into operation in recent years were first commissioned, that still means at least 15 per cent more water than at present by the year 2000. A sobering thought when we realize that it has taken 150 years to build the supply network we have in use now. Some of the new supplies will have to be from new sources, the rest by manipulating what we have already – more integrated schemes, switching from one supply or linking it up with another.

One accidental result of the inaccuracy of past population forecasts was that the effects of the 1975–6 drought were considerably less severe than they might otherwise have been. However, if the inconveniences and unnecessary expense of water shortages are to be minimized, the pressure for improved management must be kept up and the search for alternative forms of storage continued so that there are several options to choose from in the next century.

Given a choice, water engineers will undoubtedly plump for upland reservoirs if only because gravity-fed water from an upland source is bound to be cheaper than water needing extensive pumping and treatment; their first consideration must be to optimize the unit cost of the commodity they supply. It is equally certain that very few reservoir proposals will be straightforward. The greater public awareness of environmental questions means that many now question or oppose changes in land use. The concept of drowning large tracts of unspoilt countryside to form a manmade lake seems to be particularly emotive. In the lowlands, the physiographical make-up of the area will dictate large shallow reservoirs absorbing a considerable amount of prime agricultural land. This may not be true in hilly areas, where deeper reservoirs will take over less land in relation to storage volume. But even here it is the valley bottoms which contain the better-quality agricultural land, and the establishment of a reservoir fragments the farming structure of the locality by removing the sheltered land essential even to hill-farming enterprises. Another point to note is that afforestation and increased lamb production may mean water treatment costs not previously necessary further upsetting the apparent economic advantages of upland storage. Finally, reservoirs have to be built all at once; there is no possibility of stage-by-stage development – hence easing the economic impact – as there is in a groundwater scheme, for example. For all these reasons, it seems that new reservoirs will only be built where they are absolutely essential and only after rigorous examination of alternative forms of storage have been ruled out.

So what other possibilities are there? Instead of the expense of dams and the loss of useful land, why not exploit the sea: nowhere in the British Isles is more than seventy miles from the coast. Many of the Middle Eastern states use desalination plants for their freshwater supplies, much of the expertise being British-based. The objectives of any desalination process are simple, just the need to remove a 3·5 per cent salt 'impurity' from seawater, an easy technological feat. What is difficult is to make the process work without large energy demands. No one technique has yet bettered an energy input of 0·75 kilowatt per hour for each cubic metre of seawater treated, equivalent to about 3 kilowatts per 4,550 litres.

The main techniques in use are illustrated below. In both electro-dialysis and reverse osmosis the water is passed through a membrane. In electrodialysis the energy to drive the system is electrical, while in reverse osmosis the water is pushed through by physical pressure. In each case the salts are left behind the membrane. Neither process purifies all the water fed in – a proportion of pure water is abstracted, leaving a more concentrated residue behind. Both operate most efficiently when producing between 10 and 50 per cent pure water from the raw mixture. Circumstances will sometimes make one method more appropriate than the other. For example electrodialysis is used in Libya and reverse osmosis in a hotel in Colorado Springs. The hotel is sited up in the mountains and had to rely on water imported by tanker. Its freshwater now comes from its own effluent passed through a reverse osmosis process and merely topped up with tanker supply as necessary. Even in this country, despite our high energy costs, reverse osmosis is used on a small scale to treat brackish groundwaters.

Currently, reverse osmosis and freezing processes are more economic than multi-stage flash distillation. But all are costly. A few years ago a site at Ipswich was chosen for the construction of a desalination plant which would have been used in combination with existing conventional water sources. From the feasibility studies it seemed to come out as a cheaper alternative than constructing a direct supply storage reservoir. The design work went to an advanced stage before escalating costs caused the cancellation of the project. All one can say at present is that the economics of desalination are complicated because of the uncertainty of the future direction of the power supply industries; one of the often-cited spinoffs of nuclear power stations is the capacity to include distillation plant very easily.

An extra difficulty is that the concentrated brine solution which is left after the pure water has been distilled off is highly corrosive. This makes all plant very expensive to build and maintain. But at the end it is worth remembering that 'pure' water is not what is required, since in some areas brackish water is added to existing water supplies to improve that indefinable quality of palatability. It would be foolish to

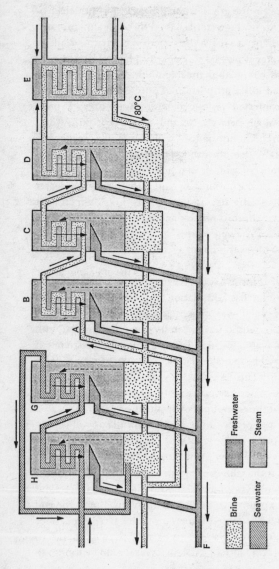

Figure 26 Various types of desalination plant.

The multistage flash-distillation process. Brine at (A) passes under pressure in the condenser coils of flash chambers (B), (C) and (D), to heat exchanger (E), and as it flows in the reverse direction, water vapour flashes off and is condensed on the cooler brine-filled coils above. The condensate forms part of the freshwater outflow at (F). The brine, now at 60°C, passes into flash chambers (G) and (H), which contain condenser coils fed with raw seawater. This is recycled into the concentrated brine of the last flash chamber and the resultant liquid is partly run off as waste and partly recycled to (A). From right to left the flash chambers operate at a progressively reduced temperature and pressure.

Freshwater

Steam

Brine

Seawater

80°C

Figure 26—*continued*

Electrodialysis. Cation membranes alternate with anion membranes in a vertical stack between the electrodes. Brackish water pumped in at (A), (B), (C) and (D) leaves as concentrate at (W) and (Y) and as partially deionized (i.e. desalinated) water at (X) and (Z). Three or four stacks are used in series to produce water of the required purity.

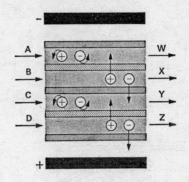

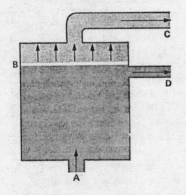

Reverse osmosis. Brackish water entering at (A) is subjected to a pressure in excess of, and in the opposing direction to, the osmotic pressure operating across the semipermeable membrane (B). Water passes through the membrane and is drawn off at (C). Brine is led away at (D).

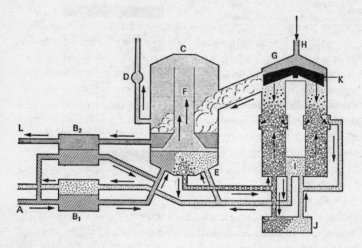

Figure 26 — *continued*

The vacuum freeze desalination process. Seawater (18°C) enters at (A), passing through the heat exchangers (B_1 and B_2) to the base of the hydroconverter (C). At a pressure of 3 millimetres mercury absolute, maintained by exhaust pump (D), the seawater mixes with freezing brine entering at (E). The brine boils, and ice crystals form in the seawater. The water vapour passes up the central funnel (F) and the ice/brine slurry passes to the base of the counterwasher (G). Pure water entering at (H) washes the salt from the ice crystals and the resulting brine passes into the central counterwasher tank (I). Some of this is recycled to the hydroconverter, and some via heat exchanger (B_1) to waste. The refrigeration plant (J) maintains the working temperature of the counterwasher. Clean ice crystals at the top of the counterwasher are conveyed by the rotating scraper (K) to the upper portion of the hydroconverter. Here the heat of condensation of the vapour provides the heat of fusion of the ice and pure water at 0°C is formed. This passes through heat exchanger (B_2) and leaves the plant at (L).

dismiss desalination as impracticable for all time simply because the energy-cost part of the economic equation will not come right just now.

Even if we rule out the possibility of using seawater, the coastline has other attractions for the water engineer. Every hour of every day huge amounts of freshwater, amounting to millions of litres a year, are washed out to sea through the estuaries of our rivers. Ambitious schemes have been put forward to build barrages across the mouths of estuaries to create large reservoirs for storing this vital water. The plans for the Wash barrages have received the most publicity because they have had the most attention in terms of feasibility study and economic appraisal but there are schemes for other estuaries, notably for barrages across the Dee, Morecambe Bay, the Solway Firth and the Humber (the area draining to the Humber is equivalent to a fifth of the total land surface of England).

Original plans for a complete barrage across the whole of the Wash were soon dismissed on grounds of cost, to be replaced with a proposal to build a barrage cutting off about half the sea. This would dam up the freshwater from the rivers Great Ouse, Nene, Welland and Witham. It would then be pumped into storage lagoons. Even this idea was eventually rejected because existing engineering expertise is not capable of meeting the necessary stringent design criteria. Instead, it was proposed to build four huge reservoirs contained by artificial banks about a mile offshore. The development of the reservoirs would cover about 500 square kilometres of the tidal fringes of the Wash and call for nine metre-high banks above sea level. The Wash scheme and other estuarial storage schemes are extremely attractive on many counts. They remove the need to destroy prime inland sites, the cost of treatment plant is similar to that already existing since only riverwater is used, and capital costs are of the order of those involved in conventional reservoir dam construction, *pro rata* for size.

Trial embankments have been built to see how they stand up to the battering of the sea. The first reservoir would be located near the outfall of the Great Ouse, water from which would be abstracted from behind a new tidal sluice to be built upstream of the port of King's Lynn. An extra sophistication is to include in the scheme a method of pumping seawater into the mouth of the river to replace the

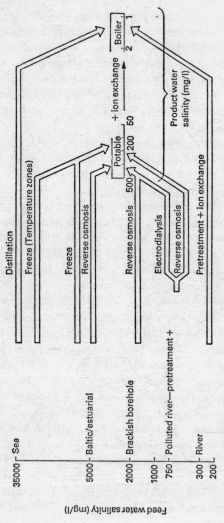

Figure 27   Schematic diagram of desalination processes and their applications.

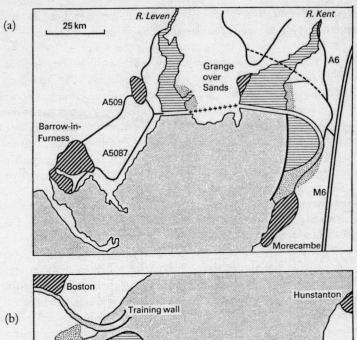

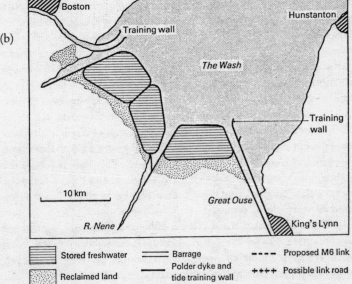

Figure 28 Proposed estuarial storage schemes for (A) Morecambe Bay (B) the Wash.

freshwater abstracted. This is necessary to dilute polluting effluents and to keep up the required minimum flow in the main channels.

A unique scheme of this sort naturally poses many questions. One concerns the ecological impact on the wild life of the area and has already led to considerable research expenditure. The abundant invertebrate fauna of the sand and mudflats of the estuary support large numbers of wading birds, and in winter the Wash is one of the two most frequented bays in Britain. The Wash also has the largest single concentration of common seals in the British Isles and is one of the most important areas for shell fish. Although researchers are fairly confident that no drastic changes will occur, there is little doubt that the removal of the mudflats and the loss of some salt and brackish water habitats inshore of the reservoir sites will alter the distribution pattern of some of the flora and fauna. Further work is needed on the tidal and sediment transport processes which will be impeded by the construction.

The Wash scheme has been shelved for the present. Although calculations show that present supplies fall short of demand, better integration of existing water sources in the area will defer the need for the Wash reservoirs for some time. Recent reappraisal of river management, in part required by the 1975–6 drought, have shown that a lot more residual flow in rivers can be made use of without harmful effects, and the experimental banks already built have success-fully removed the fear of siltation problems in the estuary. Dilution of the riverwater will be done by dredging rather than the more complicated method of recirculating seawater, and even dredging will not be required below Denver if the CEGB go ahead with their plans to build a direct-cooled power station there. This station would use seawater brought in from a deep sea intake through a tunnel under the estuary clay and discharge the wastewater into the river, thus making up the extra volume required.

It seems likely that the increased effluent releases and augmented dry weather flows which will gradually increase in the next few years with growing industrial development within the region will just about keep pace with the extra demand. It could be that by the year 2000 the flow in the rivers draining into the Wash will not be very different from the present, despite all changes.

The idea of artificially recharging major groundwater aquifers may well replace grandiose schemes such as estuarial barrages. The large aquifers under much of the south-east of England are dynamic systems. Their storage capacities continually change in response to withdrawal during the summer by evaporation and overflow through springs, and to slow replenishment during the winter from rain seeping downwards. Some aquifers such as the large tracts of sand and chalk in the London Basin have been exploited for generations, with many wells in constant operation since the eighteenth century. Abstraction in London has increased steadily with growth in population to the point where some 227 million litres per day were withdrawn between 1925 and 1940. As a result the natural ground-water levels dropped by as much as 75 metres and much of the underlying strata dewatered over an area of 900 square kilometres. Ultimately, of course, the natural discharges ceased and the springs dried up, leaving only the wells still functioning. That the level of exploitation was getting dangerously near to overkill became obvious when sulphate-rich water from the overlying clay intruded into the sand and chalk, when the flow in the streams dropped, when there were occasional traces of salty water in the wells and the ground surface subsided as the underlying clay shrank.

The total abstraction from the London Basin during the past two hundred years has been estimated at 5,080 million cubic metres. Since the early 1940s abstraction has fallen to 186 million litres per day and apparently a steady-state situation now exists. But this over-use of the aquifer has left a 'hole' behind; the dewatered rock has considerable storage capacity. If means can be found to put spare or surplus water back underground, the potential savings on reservoir storage are enormous. Exponents of the idea claim that the spare capacity of the London Basin aquifer is equivalent to seven times the volume of all the existing surface reservoirs currently providing London with water.

Although the first aquifer recharge experiments were carried out in the 1890s by the East London Water Works Company, the idea has not got far beyond the feasibility study stage. A pilot scheme to pump 36·4 million cubic metres of water into the aquifer of the lower Lea Valley started in the spring of 1977. A high-capacity pumping station at Walthamstow is linked to a line of existing abstraction wells running from Waltham Abbey to Lea Bridge and spare purification

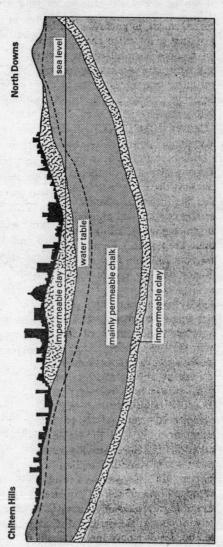

Figure 29 Abstraction of groundwater for London. A diagrammatic section through the London Basin with the vertical scale exaggerated. The aquifer, mainly Chalk, is up to 213 metres thick, and lies between two layers of impermeable clay. Rain percolates into the exposed aquifer on the Chiltern Hills and the North Downs, and flows down towards London. Groundwater was once a major source of the supply for the city but now supplies only 16 per cent of London's water.

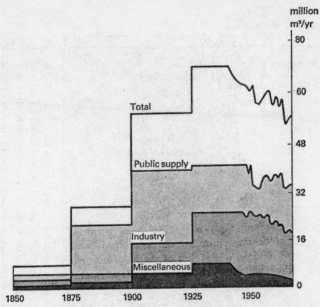

Abstraction of groundwater between 1850 and 1965.

capacity is used to treat the surplus water before it goes back underground. The Thames Water Authority hopes that up to 75 per cent of the stored water will be recoverable. But as with many other seemingly simple schemes which interfere with natural processes, a number of unresolved questions remain. The most obvious one is that of the long-term effect of adding water which will always be a few degrees warmer than the water in the aquifer into which it is being put. Are there for example likely to be any changes in the solubility of the rock matrix?

The technique is widely practised in other countries and a close watch is kept for signs of trouble. In Germany artificial recharge is extensive along the Main, Rhine, and Ruhr, all rivers with very heavy pollution loads. Riverwater is abstracted, passed through settling-beds and treated to remove suspended matter before going to infiltration basins. The Netherlands makes heavy use of the coastal sand dunes to store rainfall. Most of the country is underlain by saltwater so that the spongelike capacity of the dunes to store freshwater is especially

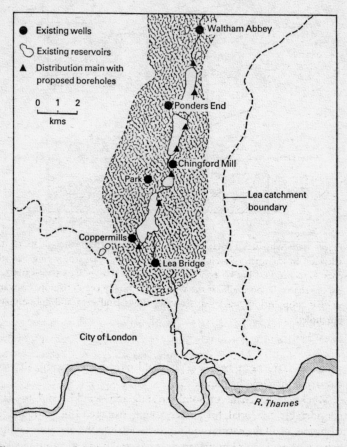

Figure 30   Artificial recharge for London. Aquifers are normally recharged by winter rains penetrating into the porous rock. In the Lea Valley of north London, an attempt is being made to recharge the aquifer artificially by pumping water into the chalk through boreholes. The shaded area shows the underground region which will be artificially recharged.

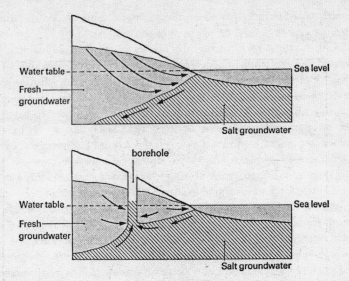

Figure 31 Saltwater contamination. The lighter freshwater floats on the saltwater in the form of a convex lens. The effect of overpumping near the coast is to produce both a cone of depression and a wedge of seawater that rises towards the borehole. If the water table finally ceases to slope seaward, or if it drops below sea level, seawater flows landward and contaminates boreholes.

valuable. Care must be taken to avoid over-pumping or saltwater comes up through the dunes.

Much of the chalk of southern England would seem to have considerable potential for underground storage. But although so common, of all the natural aquifer rocks, chalk is the one about whose behaviour geologists know least. It behaves like an enormous block of blotting paper and exhibits some peculiar aspects in connection with recharge. It is usually assumed that the reason for the rapid recovery of well levels after excessive pumping or dry summers is due to fissuring within the chalk. How the mechanism operates is not at all clear and needs much more working on. One other disturbing factor is that it is clear that the storage capacity is a function of depth, efficiency decreasing the further down one goes. If that is the case, what reliance can be placed on the geologists' estimates of the true storage capacity of the deeper parts of the aquifer?

Other aquifer rocks such as the Bunter sandstones are not usually considered for conventional groundwater exploitation because the quality of the water deteriorates badly below certain depths. However, the storage potential of the rock itself is still the same and some postulate that such rocks are eminently suitable for artificial recharge. Freshwater is stored in saline aquifers in the States and also in Israel where the policy is to divert at least 50 per cent of all surface water underground as soon as possible to minimize evaporation losses.

There are no doubt many possibilities for storing water in this way, and much borehole information already exists, a good deal of it locked up in the confidential archives of the oil companies. The advantages seem almost too good to be true. In theory at least, water can be stored without the huge capital costs and maintenance charges associated with conventional reservoirs and what is put in should stay there, out of reach of the wind and sun which evaporates so much from surface waters. Whether well-head pumping stations are less visually offensive than man-made lakes with their associated dams is a difficult question to answer; they are probably acceptable in urban surroundings but would obtrude much like electricity pylons in a rural setting.

For areas with no groundwater resources there have to be alternative plans, either for new reservoirs or for importation of surplus water from elsewhere. Some two-thirds of the extra water needed must come from transfers across the boundaries of the new regional water authorities. But these organizations have demonstrated from the first that they intend to implement the Act fully and will strive to be self-sufficient. There could be a danger here of extra money being spent through regional short-sightedness unless the idea of a national grid for water can also be fully implemented.

The old Water Resources Board on many occasions pointed out how savings could arise from the sharing of development costs for new large sites, too big for single authorities to handle. There are examples of cooperative arrangements which prove the point. The Midland cities of Sheffield, Derby, Leicester and Nottingham came together through the Derwent Valley Water Board and found that surplus water over and above their individual requirements could be produced from a joint scheme, whereas they had had barely enough when each city organized its own resources, using local facilities only. More recently the same area has benefited from the transfer of water from Empingham reservoir (now called Rutland Water), operated by the Anglian Water Authority, until their own region gets water from a new reservoir, on the River Derwent, currently being built by the Severn/Trent Water Authority.

There are unfortunately cases of inefficiency because of lack of cooperation. In 1968 a plan to drain four towns and seventy-seven villages in Dorset using a single larger diameter pipe-run foundered because the nine county district councils in the area could not agree over the costing procedures. The piecemeal arrangements made afterwards naturally cost far more per head of population served than did the original proposal. Again, the large Queen Mother reservoir at Datchet was commissioned even though adequate storage could have been made available through the utilization of the many disused gravel pits in the area. Perhaps the inter-industry bureaucratic boundaries were too hard to negotiate.

The most ambitious scheme on the stocks at present, which does go a long way towards a 'grid' solution, is undoubtedly the plan to transfer water from the River Severn to the Thames. Essentially this involves tighter control of the flow in the Severn with extra regulating reservoir capacity, so that not only can water be taken out of the Severn more extensively than at present but that water can also be transferred, first to the River Wye and secondly via a pipe through the Cotswolds to the upper tributaries of the Thames; and from there, if necessary, even into parts of East Anglia. The Londoners of the future could be drinking water which fell several days earlier in the mountains of central Wales.

The extensive research necessary has already happened. The DOE's Central Water Planning Unit completed a five-year feasibility study, part of which compared the costs of alternatives. Not only do forecasts of demands have to be scrupulously checked, and modified as new information becomes available, but the figures must also be matched to the changing pattern of resources arising from natural riverflows, artificial surface storage, groundwater stores and transfers from these sources. Any increase in yield from the projected system depends on how much it is used and on imposed control rules, the design of which has to be determined by the natural hydrology and levels of assumed demand. As an example, it is calculated that the natural flow in the Thames during dry periods would be too low to meet the projected demands of the year 2001. The deficiencies can be made good by withdrawals from the Thames surface storage reservoirs and by transfers from the Severn or from the Thames groundwater abstractions, in that order of preference.

It is now thought best to continue transfers to augment the natural riverflow throughout the winter, so that the reservoirs are refilled, and where there is any shortfall, to use groundwater abstractions. The whole scheme depends on constructing an enlarged Craig Goch reservoir to regulate the water in the Severn. The existing dam must be extended – at a cost of £40 million – and, because of the large areas the scheme will serve, the costs are to be shared between the Severn/Trent Water Authority, the main beneficiaries, and the Welsh Water Authority in whose area Craig Goch lies. But there has been no agreement about commissioning the dam as yet because of fears that the Welsh will want to charge for water 'exports', a situation not helped by the delays in devolution legislation. Until this question is resolved there will be no progress. It is currently estimated that Craig Goch water will not actually be needed before 1995 so, allowing for a ten-year construction schedule, no real action is necessary before 1985. The two authorities nevertheless sought parliamentary approval to build the 95-metre-high dam in 1978. The long-term objectives of the scheme, which will provide water for about a third of the country well into the next century, call for later raising the dam an extra 12 metres. The 1978 application related to the first stage only, so as not to jeopardize planning approval.

Meanwhile, an independent method of increasing the flow in the Thames is being examined. Though hampered by the 1975–6 drought, which put abnormal extraction pressures on the river catchment, the Thames Water Authority has nevertheless shown that it is possible to bypass the natural drainage processes to increase riverflow. Water is pumped out of the Chalk in the Berkshire Downs near Lambourn and put into the tributaries Pang and Kennet, to flow into the Thames at Caversham, the amount and timing of the pumping being related to the main river levels downstream at Teddington. This part of the plan has been put into operation. The next stage is to reverse the process, to pump back out of the rivers

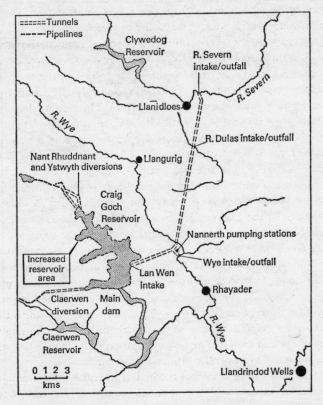

Figure 32 The Craig Goch scheme. The present reservoir, which supplies water to Birmingham, would be enlarged twenty-fold and in dry periods would release water to the Rivers Severn and Wye through tunnel aqueducts. Fully developed, Craig Goch will be the largest lake in Britain.

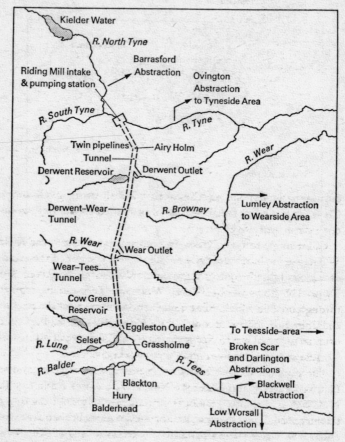

Figure 33 The Kielder Water scheme. Kielder reservoir, one of the largest man-made lakes in the country, has a surface area of 10·86 square kilometres and holds over 200 million cubic metres of water. The main dam, 52 metres high, impounds the headwaters of the River North Tyne a short distance upstream of the village of Falstone.

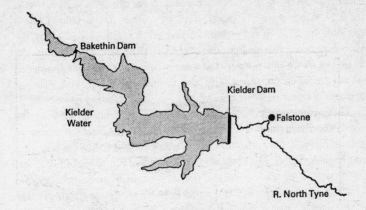

during the winter and put the excess water down the wells into the Chalk. It is expected that the groundwater input will only be used one year in every five.

Comparable to Craig Goch, in both scale and cost, is the Kielder Water scheme in the north-east. This project concerned the creation of a 1,000 hectare control reservoir at Kielder on the River North Tyne. The flows of the Rivers Wear and Tees can be regulated through use of a 29 kilometre aqueduct downstream of the reservoir, and thus provide extra water for industrial Teesside. Part of the original proposal was to transfer water from Kielder reservoir to north Yorkshire, but so far this option is not being taken up.

The problem of satisfying all parties in the sensitive areas of the National Parks is also facing the North West Water Authority. The NWWA is currently investigating four possibilities of catering for the increased demands projected for their region. Probably the most efficient in water yield is the plan to extend the area of Haweswater but it is bound to be the most fraught as far as public opinion goes. The most economical in terms of financial outlay is the building of a new reservoir either on Borrow Beck, a tributary of the River Lune, or one at Hellifield on the River Ribble. Both sites have a limited life, however. The remaining possibility is to go for estuary storage by building a barrage or artificial reservoirs within the tidal area of Morecambe Bay. The water authority is under some pressure to contribute to the Craig Goch scheme and get the extra water needed through complicated transfers. This of course may be the cheapest solution of all if water is considered on a national scale, but the authority is not too enthusiastic about this proposal. They favour the notion of being self-sufficient in their own region. The possibilities of full exploitation of rainfall in the region are good, and even of exporting water to other regions.

The crash programme known as RODEO, brought in during the 1976 drought in the dry East Anglian regions, perhaps points to a more acceptable way for future management procedures than finding new reservoir sites. RODEO stands for Reversal of Drainage of Ely Ouse. Its successful operation during the two months of September and October 1976 gained an extra 135,000 cubic metres of water per day from the Ely Ouse through the building of a temporary dam and the installing of pumps at each of seven locks up to the intake of the large reservoir of Graffham Water. Half the water saved was pumped each day from behind the new dam and put back over each lock to the intake point to Graffham Water. This had the effect of reversing the flow of the Ely Ouse for the 35 kilometre stretch between Earith and Denver sluice, drawing back the natural drainage of the flat fenland countryside. The other 67,500 cubic metres came from abstracting the full natural flow of the Ouse at Offerd, a special Drought Order being needed to allow the flow to the Ouse estuary to fall to virtually zero. All told, these operations supplied about 10 per cent of the regional water authority's demands during the dry period and kept the huge Graffham Water reservoir at the 30 per cent full mark until the winter recharge began to take effect in the autumn.

Although an extremely cheap scheme as far as such projects go, there was unfortunately a very high cost in terms of loss of amenity. The situation at King's Lynn was described as ghastly at the point where the effluents from the town's sewerage and the British Sugar Corporation's sugar beet plant discharged into the virtually dry estuary. A short-term solution was to improve treatment facilities at the sewage works and to get BSC's factory to cut its effluent discharge by a third, flushing it out only twice daily. Some of the normal downstream water intakes naturally had to be abandoned because of the deteriorating quality of the water (but this loss was made good by the savings made upstream through Graffham Water storage). Despite the nuisances caused by the limits put on abstraction, RODEO is an interesting experiment, relying as it does purely on the existing river channels. Had it been put into operation earlier in the year the savings would have been more, since the water would have been intercepted before losses from evaporation and seepage through the base of the tributary rivers could take effect. The reason it was left until later in the season was the heavy regional demand for irrigation water, normally abstracted directly from the rivers.

During the last ten years or so, as water resource schemes have got bigger in scope and complexity, many researchers have tried to assess their impact on the natural environment and to predict how river regimes may alter through the management practices being imposed. Studies of complete river basins, with or without storages such as lakes or man-made reservoirs, have been carried out in many parts of the world, including the UK. In the last century the rapid development of the land by both developers and railway engineers demanded methods of calculating the dimensions of bridges, culverts and drainage ditches able to cope with the runoff likely during any particular year or storm event. So basin studies or catchment research was born, whereby complete drainage basins or river catchment areas (what the Americans call watersheds) are instrumented to gain records of gross input (rainfall) to be compared with output (streamflow) and the estimated losses from evaporation, soil moisture storage or recharge of groundwater. Quite early on it became clear that different types of basin behaved differently, not only according to their geology, which affects the soil part of the hydrological cycle, but also according to the type of vegetation cover or land use.

This question of land use has considerable implications for water resources management. Traditionally, water authorities were encouraged to plant trees round storage reservoirs to prevent trespass and erosion of soil, both of which might cause a decline in quality and quantity of water stored. It was strongly believed that coniferous forest reduces both the incidence and magnitude of floods. But in 1956 a water engineer gave a paper at a scientific meeting in which he claimed that the trees growing round his reservoir were using more water than would grass or other short vegetation, to the extent that he felt the Forestry Commission ought to pay a levy for the reduced yield of the reservoir. The storm of protest this paper provoked led to the setting up of paired catchment experiments in upland Wales to assess the validity of the claims, particularly since results from other parts of the world with similar climates are conflicting.

The Institute of Hydrology, one of the organizations of the Natural Environment Research Council, has a long-term, on-going catchment experiment at Plynlimon, a few miles inland behind Aberystwyth, comparing the runoff or water yield of the headwaters of the Rivers Wye and Severn. Arising in adjacent valleys the two rivers are remarkably similar in that they share the same geology, topography, aspect and climate. The difference between the two is that the Wye rises on land used for sheep grazing and therefore supporting a mixture of grass, rushes and bracken while the Severn runs through Forestry Commission land and a large part of the catchment is covered with dense conifer plantation. Simultaneous measurements of rainfall, water storage, water losses and riverflow in both catchments indicate the effect of the trees. Comparison of the runoff volumes from the two catchments show a significant 'loss' from the Severn which, when adjusted to relate the runoff to the tree-covered area alone, is considerably more than would be expected from the conventional water balance calculations normally used for water resource assessment.

The reasons are not hard to find. The trees do not use more water in a biological sense but rather that there are stronger aerodynamic forces operating over forest canopies than nearer the ground and thus much more efficient removal of the water caught by the foliage or being transpired through the leaf pores. The implications of the interception factor are difficult to assess. There can be no doubt that in summers such as those of the 1970s, a 20 per cent loss of potential storage because reservoir catchments have extensive tree cover is something which has to be taken into account. The water 'lost' each year from the forested Severn catchment through this interception process is enough to meet the annual water needs of a town of forty-three thousand people. The experimental catchment covers a mere 10 square kilometres, an insignificant proportion of the area draining into the nearby Clyweddog reservoir, for example. Alternatively, the 20 per cent evaporation loss can be thought of as equivalent to 19 per cent of the volume of the same reservoir, which holds over 50 million cubic metres.

Just as important has been the study of the way catchments have responded when a drought broke. If the trees are exerting any kind of delaying influence then the vital recharge mechanisms are also slowed down, with the possibility of a shortfall in expected yield in future seasons. Planners working to close limits in areas where there is no margin for error will need to alter their water balance calculations accordingly. But in operational terms, of course, no engineer normally works to such critical limits. Reservoirs are not designed to be completely emptied every year.

Forestry in upland marginal areas brings precious jobs and improved access to areas with dwindling populations, not to be dismissed lightly, any more than the value of homegrown timber. However, someone has to weigh up the advantages when choosing between wood, wool or water, for they are mutually exclusive. The evaporation losses from forests are greatest at high altitudes where rainfall is heaviest and the winds blow strongest. It may be that a compromise land-use strategy will emerge, with afforestation only proceeding up to given limits in these upland areas, so that timber production is maximized without jeopardizing projected water yields.

Scientists have always been unhappy about catchment experiments because however well they quantify changes in runoff or evaporation from different areas they can never say why or how such differences take place. The Plynlimon experiment is just such a case in point and clearly the interception process needs to be examined very closely. Where for instance does the energy for the increased evaporation come from, and do all tree species behave in the same way? Until such phenomena are clearly understood the chances of using such experimental results in an operational sense are nil, for no one would dare to extrapolate from a single experimental site.

There is now a detailed study of the physics of evaporation from trees going on elsewhere, in the dry flat forests of East Anglia. Thetford Chase provides an experimental site which climatically and topographically is almost as different from Plynlimon as it is possible to get in this country. Interestingly though, the crucial result is the same: at both sites evaporation from wet forest canopies is considerably greater than from short vegetation such as grass. For the low rainfall areas of the east this is an insignificant phenomenon in water resource terms but the Thetford results have helped to emphasize the importance of evaporation loss in areas where the surface of vegetation is wet for long periods.

The end product of all such hydrological research is a mathematical-physical description (or 'model') of river basin behaviour to improve on the crudely empirical water balance approach engineers have had to work with in the past. The extension of such modelling techniques to the point when the true relationship between incoming rainfall and the ensuing streamflow is known, taking account of all the factors which influence the process, is still a long way off. But the mathematical models that do exist now are the day-to-day tools of the resource planning engineers. They allow them to consider the implications and effects of a variety of seasonal and operating conditions on their basic resource. This is fine for routine management but no operational contingency procedures can be considered fully tested until the most extreme conditions envisaged do actually happen.

There were prime examples of such failures during the 1976 drought. Conjunctive-use schemes rely on releases from regulating reservoirs in the headwater regions to maintain minimum prescribed flows in the rivers. In the summer of 1976 the water stored in the Clyweddog reservoir upstream of Newtown was held in reserve as stocks elsewhere in the Severn catchment dwindled. Clyweddog was built some ten years previously (at a cost of £6 million) for just such emergency use. Finally, there came the point in July when the first ever major release had to be authorized. The water coursing down through the dry river valley disappeared fast. The releases from Clyweddog were designed to relate to flow levels at Bewdley but the water simply never arrived there; all that happened was that the parched water meadows lining the banks of the Severn took on a new lease of life.

Likewise, the borehole water from the Chalk at Lambourn in the upper Thames Valley did not get even as far as the river junction at Caversham, though the pumping rates were supposed to restore the levels far downstream at Teddington. The much publicized Thames 'leak' from the stretch below Oxford, although found to be partly due to faults in accurate flow gauging at such abnormally low levels, was also partly due to seepage through the gravel beds in the Dorchester

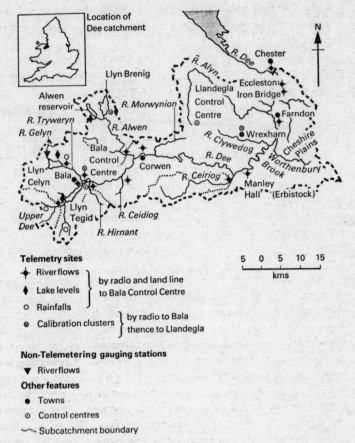

Figure 34   The Dee catchment.

area – something that happened all year round but which only showed up when the base flow in the river was down to such an all-time low. These problems of transmission loss had largely been ignored in the past. No doubt they will be incorporated into operational rules in the future now that their significance has been so effectively demonstrated in a time of stress when every litre counted.

Most management schemes are designed to operate within the spectrum of seasonal variation only, but even here an element of forecasting is necessary, particularly where flood warning is crucial. The Dee catchment in north Wales has several reservoirs both for direct water supply and to regulate the flow in the river, either to absorb excess winter runoff and alleviate possible flooding or to augment low summer flows. The final abstraction point way downstream for the town of Chester comes after the river has passed through rich agricultural land, far too valuable to be allowed to flood whenever this can be avoided. The management system which operates on the Dee has then to cope with two diametrically opposed control policies: to keep the reservoirs full enough to meet all water supply demand and empty enough to absorb excess flood water. This makes the control of the sluices extremely exacting, so much so that the Dee has been the subject of one of the most advanced experimental management systems in the world.

In the initial experimental phase, rainfall information came to the control centre at Bala from a radar scanner sited up in the mountains at Llandegla. The radar-produced image was presented on a television monitor displaying a grid network of the area covered by the radar beam, each square in the network being colour-coded according to the rainfall intensity at that moment. The 'picture' was updated every fifteen minutes, making it easy to follow the route and intensity of incoming rain storms.* Water levels in the five reservoirs of the catchment and in the river itself, downstream at the last intake point, are monitored by telemetry. The optimum control of the sluices depends on incorporating this knowledge of the state of the catchment into predictions of future flows hours or even days ahead, the simulation models being run on a computer.

So far, such forecasting has had to depend on extrapolation from current information of climatic variables. And so it is likely to remain, since meteorology has not yet advanced sufficiently to possess accurate methods of quantitative long-term weather forecasting. At the moment we have only studies of trends in temperature, rainfall, etc., to work with, from which attempts are made to extrapolate forwards. There is of course no evidence whatever that the success rate is higher than pure chance, as this type of work is based on the unproved hypothesis that the future will mirror the past.

*This radar input has now been discontinued, since the system works just as well with data coming from the cheaper-to-maintain rain-gauge network.

Those planning the efficient use of upland marginal areas in the UK have four options – sheep farming, mineral or water extraction, forestry and recreation. Even as water resource management gets more efficient, advances are being made in agriculture for the highlands. Plant-breeding experts continually stress that replanting with more productive grasses, the elimination of competition from bracken and the continual application of fertilizers would have spectacular effects on the quality of the grazing and hence on stock productivity, thus combating the inherent disadvantage of a severe climate. Forestry yields too can be improved by fertilizer application. All of which can only increase pressure for more research into growing nitrate levels. It may be that future generations will be concerned more about quality than quantity from upland areas in connection with regulating reservoirs and inter-basin transfers, because pollution at the source can endanger a vast area.

There is another kind of land-use change which has implications for both quality and quantity. Between 1951 and 1970 about 3,200 square kilometres of land were converted from agricultural to urban use. Now, about 9 per cent of the total land area of Great Britain (299,900 square kilometres) is classed as urban, marginally more than the area occupied by woods and forests. Studies of selected plots which have changed from being completely natural to fully urbanized over a twenty-year period show that the frequency of summer floods has increased markedly. The effect of urbanization is to cover the soil surface with vast tracts of impervious concrete, off which the water runs extremely fast, putting severe strain on the capacity of storm sewers instead of infiltrating the soil slowly. Increased loads of sediment and debris from runoff in areas with heavy building activity do not help the efficiency with which sewers can carry away surplus water.

Variations in water quality between different rivers exist even without any interference by mankind. Recent work on the changing temperature patterns in Devon rivers show that not only do some of the upland streams have a temperature range which varies between 4 and 5°C in a single day, but also that annual and diurnal cycles fluctuate apparently unrelated to the existing weather pattern of the period. On top of this it is also quite clear that natural temperatures can be upset easily, for example by the clearing away of trees which shaded the stream. So, one wonders, what will be the significance of temperature change in river transfers or regulating reservoirs? Under both these operational techniques large slugs of water of different temperature will be added to existing rivers and be expected to mix with the residual flow of the parent stream.

Most of the concern is over the possible effects on the native organisms of the river. Any physiological upset to the bacteria, for example, would have serious repercussions on the normal self-purifying mechanisms which operate in rivers. This is an area where there are still many unknowns. Fish stocks certainly might be affected, at least with changed distribution patterns, for it is known that fish react to changes in velocity, turbidity, dissolved oxygen content, pH, conductivity, as well as temperature, all parameters related to water discharge. Some would also claim fish susceptibility to wind speed and direction, air temperature, barometric pressure and phases of the moon, but there is as yet little scientific evidence for the latter. Apart from the upset to fish stocks which might be caused by intermittent releases changing flow velocity conditions, resident populations might also suffer through the inadvertent introduction of predator species into spawning areas or through the spread of fish diseases and parasites.

Bringing quality changes back to more mundane levels, it has already been demonstrated that changes in background concentrations of some naturally occurring solutes have unwelcome side effects on supply pipes. The area round Hillingdon has its water variously supplied from either surface reservoirs or from groundwater abstraction, depending on the current demand and storage situation. This change from one type of water to another has caused corrosion in some of the supply pipe network and the embarrassed local water company has been faced with paying the laundry bills presented by annoyed customers.

8 Conclusion

More than half the structures and plant in use today for water supply was built so long ago that it has been written off financially. The lower interest rates on borrowed capital allowed our forebears to build grandly and imaginatively, creating facilities that would be prohibitively expensive today but which had and have low running costs. They still function and we enjoy the benefits. The altered structure of the business world means that now we rely on cheaper plant and accept higher running costs, forced upon us politically because current Treasury discount rates favour high-revenue, low-capital solutions. This approach means we maintain the present standard of living at the expense of long-term investment.

Many are now questioning the upward spiral in demand for resources that our society advocates. As closer scrutiny is given to the need for energy supplied by non-renewable fossil fuels, so too is it time to look at what it costs us to provide unlimited water supplies. For although the water comes for free, moving it about has to be paid for. This is much too costly except where gravity can be the driving force; extensive pumping facilities are perhaps a luxury we cannot afford. This is the key to the universal rejection of the notion of transferring water from Scotland, where the plentiful rainfall of the Highlands provides far more water than is needed for the sparse population of the region. Even if we get to the point at which daily deliveries of potable water arrive on our doorstep alongside the morning pinta, the export of Scottish water is a non-starter.

The absolute confidence with which we can drink a glass of water drawn from the kitchen tap is a wonderful extravagance. Our water-intensive way of life means that about two tonnes of water are delivered to each household each week, virtually all of which needs to be taken away again soon afterwards. The more extensive a supply system we have, the more must it be matched by an equally comprehensive sewerage system. And more sewers means more and more water treatment plant if we intend to protect our rivers. What few people realize is that disposal costs about twice as much as water supply. This is because the pipes have to be deeper to make the flow work by gravity and sewage treatment is more expensive than natural water treatment simply because the water is dirtier.

Is it so silly then to think about splitting off the supply of the few litres of really first-class drinking water from the few hundred litres of not-so-clean water for all other uses? The answer is quite clear when we look at the costs. First, because so much of the cost of water is in the distribution mains rather than in the resource or the treatment works, the extra cost of a duplicate system of pipes far outweighs the potential savings. Dual-pipe systems do in fact exist in Teesside but although the overall supply costs are marginally lower, the quantity supplied remains the same, making the net gain minimal. Secondly, the household distribution costs of bottled water would be more than the total cost of domestic water supply (this is based on a comparison of daily milk supply costs which are currently running at 50p per household, excluding the cost of the milk). The most important consideration of all, however, must be that the 'second-rate' water will still have to be of a high enough standard to allow for accidental consumption due to misuse or cross connections.

Some engineers now query whether such grandiose schemes as Craig Goch or Kielder are really necessary. The 1975–6 drought not only showed how easy it was to economize but also forced the various water authorities to tidy up the weak points in their distribution systems. A great deal was done to relieve areas from the threat of standpipes simply by the judicious installation of new pipelines connecting different sources together, either linking reservoirs or making it possible to have standby groundwater supplies on-line. The sense of urgency persisted even into the very wet autumn and many authorities are confident that the panic measures of that summer will not be needed again. The adjustment in the legal situation to allow the water authorities to bring in tight control measures and adjustments to minimum flow levels in rivers at an early date in the season also helps to mitigate against the severity of a similar climatic situation in the future.

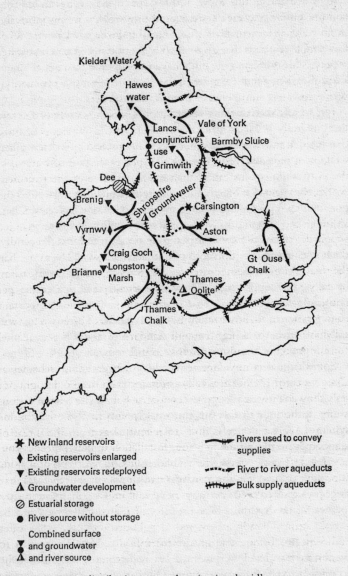

Figure 35   Water distribution network or 'national grid'.

As the demand for water was so effectively reduced through intensive publicity campaigns during the drought, it is now seriously proposed that a permanent campaign should be set in motion to discipline the market for all time. A £3 million a year advertising budget could yield a £50 million capital investment saving. Such demand management, the attempt to balance optimum production levels against the costs incurred in manufacture and distribution, is an accepted technique in other industries but so far has received scant attention in the public utilities.

Given that projected demand, set at whatever level we choose, can in fact be met in the future, there still remains the problem of what level of reliability to achieve. In the past the usual assessment of reliable yield of reservoirs was set against conditions which might occur twice in a century. As we know only too well, this did not mean that demands were met in full ninety-eight years out of a hundred, or that supplies failed in only two years out of a hundred. Does the public accept such criteria for the supply for which they pay?

If you ask the water industry for their views you find they have already made their decision. There is an almost total preoccupation with just two problems, how to get more clean water out of the existing system and how to do it using less people. These two factors really boil down to one and the same thing – shortage of money. Even the seriousness of the 1976 drought could not relieve the existing no-growth situation in water resources development; in the winter following the drought there was a moratorium placed on all capital works relating to new supply. The National Water Council said openly at the time that it was just not economic sense to invest in making supplies more certain. It was admitted that reliability could be improved so that rationing becomes less likely, but in the long term they felt it better to ask the public to accept occasional supply restrictions than higher water charges. And if they cannot increase the water rates they have to find ways of cutting back on manpower: the Thames Water Authority alone spends over £70 million a year on wages.

There is no denying that greater reliability could be achieved at a cost and if the demand were there. Two analogies are available to help us decide between these two factors. One is the signalling and points system on the railways in this country. The half-dozen days in a year when chaos reigns because of severe frost or snow is the price we pay for a system cheaper than those operating in colder climes. The second case is the electricity industry, where it has been written into the legislation of that industry that a supply shall be available at all times. If the public would accept the occasional 'brown-out' when peak loads come into operation, our power supply bills would be considerably less. The technological skills are available for a water supply of either kind; the choice between them is ours.

Index

FOR THE BEST IN PAPERBACKS, LOOK FOR THE

In every corner of the world, on every subject under the sun, Penguin represents quality and variety – the very best in publishing today.

For complete information about books available from Penguin – including Pelicans, Puffins, Peregrines and Penguin Classics – and how to order them, write to us at the appropriate address below. Please note that for copyright reasons the selection of books varies from country to country.

In the United Kingdom: Please write to *Dept E.P., Penguin Books Ltd, Harmondsworth, Middlesex, UB7 0DA*

In the United States: Please write to *Dept BA, Penguin, 299 Murray Hill Parkway, East Rutherford, New Jersey 07073*

In Canada: Please write to *Penguin Books Canada Ltd, 2801 John Street, Markham, Ontario L3R 1B4*

In Australia: Please write to the *Marketing Department, Penguin Books Australia Ltd, P.O. Box 257, Ringwood, Victoria 3134*

In New Zealand: Please write to the *Marketing Department, Penguin Books (NZ) Ltd, Private Bag, Takapuna, Auckland 9*

In India: Please write to *Penguin Overseas Ltd, 706 Eros Apartments, 56 Nehru Place, New Delhi, 110019*

In Holland: Please write to *Penguin Books Nederland B.V., Postbus 195, NL–1380AD Weesp, Netherlands*

In Germany: Please write to *Penguin Books Ltd, Friedrichstrasse 10–12, D–6000 Frankfurt Main 1, Federal Republic of Germany*

In Spain: Please write to *Longman Penguin España, Calle San Nicolas 15, E–28013 Madrid, Spain*

In France: Please write to *Penguin Books Ltd, 39 Rue de Montmorency, F-75003, Paris, France*

In Japan: Please write to *Longman Penguin Japan Co Ltd, Yamaguchi Building, 2–12–9 Kanda Jimbocho, Chiyoda-Ku, Tokyo 101, Japan*

FOR THE BEST IN PAPERBACKS, LOOK FOR THE 🐧

A CHOICE OF PENGUINS AND PELICANS

Metamagical Themas Douglas R. Hofstadter

A new mind-bending bestseller by the author of *Gödel, Escher, Bach*.

The Body Anthony Smith

A completely updated edition of the well-known book by the author of *The Mind*. The clear and comprehensive text deals with everything from sex to the skeleton, sleep to the senses.

How to Lie with Statistics Darrell Huff

A classic introduction to the ways statistics can be used to prove *anything*, the book is both informative and 'wildly funny' – *Evening News*

The Penguin Dictionary of Computers Anthony Chandor and others

An invaluable glossary of over 300 words, from 'aberration' to 'zoom' by way of 'crippled lead-frog tests' and 'output bus drivers'.

The Cosmic Code Heinz R. Pagels

Tracing the historical development of quantum physics, the author describes the baffling and seemingly lawless world of leptons, hadrons, gluons and quarks and provides a lucid and exciting guide for the layman to the world of infinitesimal particles.

The Blind Watchmaker Richard Dawkins

'Richard Dawkins has updated evolution' – *The Times* 'An enchantingly witty and persuasive neo-Darwinist attack on the anti-evolutionists, pleasurably intelligible to the scientifically illiterate' – Hermione Lee in Books of the Year, *Observer*

Asimov's New Guide to Science   Isaac Asimov

A fully updated edition of a classic work – far and away the best one-volume survey of all the physical and biological sciences.

Relativity for the Layman   James A. Coleman

Of this book Albert Einstein said: 'Gives a really clear idea of the problem, especially the development of our knowledge concerning the propagation of light and the difficulties which arose from the apparently inevitable introduction of the ether.'

The Double Helix   James D. Watson

Watson's vivid and outspoken account of how he and Crick discovered the structure of DNA (and won themselves a Nobel Prize) – one of the greatest scientific achievements of the century.

Ever Since Darwin   Stephen Jay Gould

'Stephen Gould's writing is elegant, erudite, witty, coherent and forceful' – Richard Dawkins in *Nature*

Mathematical Magic Show   Martin Gardner

A further mind-bending collection of puzzles, games and diversions by the undisputed master of recreational mathematics.

Silent Spring   Rachel Carson

The brilliant book which provided the impetus for the ecological movement – and has retained its supreme power to this day.

FOR THE BEST IN PAPERBACKS, LOOK FOR THE

A CHOICE OF PENGUINS AND PELICANS

Genetic Engineering for Almost Everybody   William Bains

Now that the 'genetic engineering revolution' has most certainly arrived, we all need to understand the ethical and practical implications of genetic engineering. Written in accessible language, they are set out in this major new book.

Brighter than a Thousand Suns   Robert Jungk

'By far the most interesting historical work on the atomic bomb I know of' – C. P. Snow

Turing's Man   J. David Bolter

We live today in a computer age, which has meant some startling changes in the ways we understand freedom, creativity and language. This major book looks at the implications.

Einstein's Universe   Nigel Calder

'A valuable contribution to the de-mystification of relativity' – *Nature*

The Creative Computer   Donald R. Michie and Rory Johnston

Computers *can* create the new knowledge we need to solve some of our most pressing human problems; this path-breaking book shows how.

Only One Earth   Barbara Ward and Rene Dubos

An extraordinary document which explains with eloquence and passion how we should go about 'the care and maintenance of a small planet'.